Resource Allocation: Managing Money and People

by
M. Scott Norton
Larry K. Kelly

D0072094

EYE ON EDUCATION
6 Depot Way West, Suite 106
Larchmont, N.Y. 10538

ISBN 1-883001-35-8

Library of Congress Cataloging-in-Publication Data

```
Norton, M. Scott.
   Resource allocation : managing money and people / by M. Scott
Norton and Larry K. Kelly.
      p.   cm. -- (School leadership library)
   Includes bibliographical references (p. ).
   ISBN 1-883001-35-8
   1. School management and organization--United States. 2. School
personnel management--United States. 3. Public schools--United
States--Business management.   I. Kelly, Larry K., 1936-   .
II. Title.  III. Series.
LB2805.N73  1997
371.2'00973--dc21                                      97-4940
                                                          CIP
```

Editorial and production services provided by:
Bookwrights
1211 Courtland Drive
Raleigh, NC 27604

Published by Eye On Education

LEADERSHIP
ADMINISTRATOR'S GUIDE TO SCHOOL-COMMUNITY RELATIONS
by George E. Pawlas

THE EDUCATOR'S BRIEF GUIDE TO COMPUTERS IN THE SCHOOLS
by Eugene F. Provenzo, Jr.

HANDS-ON LEADERSHIP TOOLS FOR PRINCIPALS
by Raymond Calabrese, Gary Short, and Sally Zepeda

INSTRUCTION AND THE LEARNING ENVIRONMENT
by James W. Keefe and John M. Jenkins

INTERPERSONAL SENSITIVITY
by John R. Hoyle and Harry M. Crenshaw

LEADERSHIP: A RELEVANT AND REALISTIC ROLE FOR PRINCIPALS
by Gary M. Crow, L. Joseph Matthews, and Lloyd E. McCleary

LEADERSHIP THROUGH COLLABORATION:
ALTERNATIVES TO THE HIERARCHY
by Michael Koehler and Jeanne C. Baxter

MOTIVATING OTHERS: CREATING THE CONDITIONS
by David P. Thompson

ORAL AND NONVERBAL EXPRESSION
by Ivan Muse

ORGANIZATIONAL OVERSIGHT:
PLANNING AND SCHEDULING FOR EFFECTIVENESS
by David A. Erlandson, Peggy L. Stark, and Sharon M. Ward

THE PRINCIPAL'S EDGE
by Jack McCall

SYSTEMIC REFORM
BLOCK SCHEDULING: A CATALYST FOR CHANGE IN HIGH SCHOOLS
by Robert Lynn Canady and Michael D. Rettig

DIRECTORY OF INNOVATIONS IN ELEMENTARY SCHOOLS
by Jane McCarthy and Suzanne Still

EDUCATIONAL TECHNOLOGY: BEST PRACTICES FROM
AMERICA'S SCHOOLS
by William C. Bozeman and Donna J. Baumbach

INNOVATIONS IN PARENT AND FAMILY INVOLVEMENT
by J. William Rioux and Nancy Berla

RESEARCH ON EDUCATIONAL INNOVATIONS
by Arthur K. Ellis and Jeffrey T. Fouts

RESEARCH ON SCHOOL RESTRUCTURING
by Arthur K. Ellis and Jeffrey T. Fouts

THE SCHOOL PORTFOLIO:
A COMPREHENSIVE FRAMEWORK FOR SCHOOL IMPROVEMENT
by Victoria L. Bernhardt

SCHOOLS FOR ALL LEARNERS: BEYOND THE BELL CURVE
by Renfro C. Manning

SCHOOL-TO-WORK
by Arnold H. Packer and Marion W. Pines

QUALITY AND EDUCATION: CRITICAL LINKAGES
by Betty L. McCormick

TRANSFORMING EDUCATION THROUGH TOTAL
QUALITY MANAGEMENT: A PRACTITIONER'S GUIDE
by Franklin P. Schargel

TEACHING AND LEARNING
BRINGING THE NCTM STANDARDS TO LIFE:
BEST PRACTICES FROM ELEMENTARY EDUCATORS
by Lisa B. Owen and Charles E. Lamb

THE EDUCATOR'S GUIDE TO IMPLEMENTING OUTCOMES
By William J. Smith

HANDBOOK OF EDUCATIONAL TERMS AND APPLICATIONS
by Arthur K. Ellis and Jeffrey T. Fouts

MATHEMATICS THE WRITE WAY:
ACTIVITIES FOR EVERY ELEMENTARY CLASSROOM
by Marilyn S. Neil

THE PERFORMANCE ASSESSMENT HANDBOOK
Volume 1 Portfolios and Socratic Seminars
Volume 2 Performances and Exhibitions
by Bil Johnson

TEACHING IN THE BLOCK: STRATEGIES FOR ENGAGING
ACTIVE LEARNER
by Robert Lynn Canady and Michael D. Rettig

FOREWORD

The School Leadership Library was designed to show practicing and aspiring principals what they should know and be able to do to be effective leaders of their schools. The books in this series were written to answer the question, "How can we improve our schools by improving the effectiveness of our principals?"

Success in the principalship, like in other professions, requires mastery of a knowledge and skills base. One of the goals of the National Policy Board for Educational Administration (sponsored by NAESP, NASSP, AASA, ASCD, NCPEA, UCEA, and other professional organizations) was to define and organize that knowledge and skill base. The result of our efforts was the development of a set of 21 "domains," building blocks representing the core understandings and capabilities required of successful principals.

The 21 domains of knowledge and skills are organized under four broad areas: Functional, Programmatic, Interpersonal and Contextual. They are as follows:

FUNCTIONAL DOMAINS
Leadership
Information Collection
Problem Analysis
Judgment
Organizational Oversight
Implementation
Delegation

PROGRAMMATIC DOMAINS
Instruction and the Learning
  Environment
Curriculum Design
Student Guidance and Devel-
  opment
Staff Development
Measurement and Evaluation
Resource Allocation

INTERPERSONAL DOMAINS
Motivating Others
Interpersonal Sensitivity
Oral and Nonverbal Expres-
  sion
Written Expression

CONTEXTUAL DOMAINS
Philosophical and Cultural
  Values
Legal and Regulatory Appli-
  cations
Policy and Political Influences
Public Relations

These domains are not discrete, separate entities. Rather, they evolved only for the purpose of providing manageable descriptions of essential content and practice so as to better understand the entire complex role of the principalship. Because human behavior comes in "bunches" rather than neat packages, they are also overlapping pieces of a complex puzzle. Consider the domains as converging streams of behavior that spill over one another's banks but that all contribute to the total reservoir of knowledge and skills required of today's principals.

The School Leadership Library was established by General Editors David Erlandson and Al Wilson to provide a broad examination of the content and skills in all of the domains. The authors of each volume in this series offer concrete and realistic illustrations and examples, along with reflective exercises. You will find their work to be of exceptional merit, illustrating with insight the depth and interconnectedness of the domains. This series provides the fullest, most contemporary, and most useful information available for the preparation and professional development of principals.

> Scott D. Thomson
> Executive Secretary
> National Policy Board for
> Educational Administration

If you would like information about how to become a member of the **School Leadership Library**, please contact

Eye On Education
Suite 106
6 Depot Way West
Larchmont, NY 10538
(914) 833-0551
(914) 833-0761 FAX

About the Authors

Dr. M. Scott Norton, a former teacher, assistant superinten-
dent, and superintendent, is currently Professor of Educational
Administration and Supervision at Arizona State University in
Tempe.

Dr. Norton is the co-author of two leading books in their
respective fields: HUMAN RESOURCE ADMINISTRATION:
PERSONNEL ISSUES AND NEEDS (Webb, Montello and
Norton) and THE SCHOOL SUPERINTENDENT: NEW RE-
SPONSIBILITIES, NEW LEADERSHIP (Norton, Webb, Dlugosh,
and Sybouts). He has received several awards honoring his ser-
vice and contributions to the field of educational administra-
tion from such organizations as the University Council for
Educational Administration, the Arizona Educational Research
Organization, and several others.

Dr. Larry K. Kelly is a former classroom teacher, principal,
personnel director and assistant superintendent for human resources. During his sixteen years as a campus administrator, he
had primary responsibility for the management and monitoring of the school budget.

Dr. Kelly currently serves as the Director of Professional Development for the Arizona School Administrators Association.

PREFACE

If quality leadership is to occur, principals must understand the most effective and efficient ways to allocate resources. Yet, until recently, resource allocation had not been presented in a coherent, interrelated fashion. School leaders have historically dealt with finance, personnel, facilities, material and time as separate considerations. Such separation changed in 1993 when the National Policy Board for Educational Administration did an analysis of principal functions and grouped them into 21 clusters with resource allocation being one.

Many organizations and agencies have grappled with the arduous undertaking of re-engineering the role of the principal. NCATE, a national accrediting agency, has expected that teaching and learning about resource allocation will be examined, in context, under the four basic leadership headings of Strategic, Instructional, Political and Community, and Organizational. Many evaluators working with NCATE are calling for an integrated curriculum.

In addition to the work of the National Policy Board and NCATE, external agencies such as the Danforth Foundation, and most recently the Council of Chief State School Officials, have addressed ways to raise standards for principals. Efforts have been launched by training and development organizations and by forward-thinking departments of educational administration and leadership.

Historic policy changes and legislation have been enacted by governmental agencies, such as the North Carolina Assembly in 1993 and the Kansas State School Board in 1997 to change licensure and certification. More emphasis is being placed on demonstrated learning, in context, for initial licensure. Demonstrated practice and ongoing professional development are being required for certification. Considerable emphasis is now being placed on the results of learning with less on classes taken. Ongoing professional growth and development are expected.

Principals are being prepared to engage in a race without a finish line. The expectations for unending improvement and achieving ever-higher standards are becoming the norm. To improve education, principals must have functional knowledge at their fingertips. Such knowledge must be easily accessed and presented in a digestible format. This volume, *Resource Allocation: Managing Money and People*, is an exceptional resource for this quest.

The National Policy Board describes resource allocation as "Procuring, apportioning, monitoring, accounting for and evaluating fiscal, human, material, and time resources to reach outcomes that reflect the needs and goals of the school site; planning and developing the budget process with appropriate staff." With a commitment to writing a usable volume, Norton and Kelly have addressed each element of the Board's definition. With a clear and practical writing style, they convey knowledge and understanding of key components to success.

Resource Allocation: Managing Money and People is a practical resource that may easily be used by school leaders. The authors understand their audience and have made it user friendly with "real world" applications of merit.

David A. Erlandson
Alfred P. Wilson

TABLE OF CONTENTS

1 FINANCING THE SCHOOL PROGRAM 1
   A PHILOSOPHY AND BELIEF SYSTEM 3
      RESOURCES AVAILABLE TO THE PRINCIPAL 10
   TYPES AND SOURCES OF FINANCIAL RESOURCES 14
      LOCAL AND NON-LOCAL FUNDS 14
      COMPETITIVE GRANTS 16
      FOUNDATION FUNDS 16
      SCHOOL BUSINESS PARTNERSHIPS FUNDS 16
      STUDENT ACTIVITY FUNDS 17
      FACILITY RENTAL FUNDS 17
   FORCES IMPACTING ON THE ALLOCATION OF FUNDS TO THE
      SCHOOL 18
   FORCES IMPACTING THE UTILIZATION OF FINANCIAL
      RESOURCES 21
      FEDERAL AND STATE GRANTS 21
      EMPLOYEE AGREEMENTS OR CONTRACTS 23
      CASE LAW 23
      STATE AND FEDERAL STATUTE 24
      ORGANIZATIONAL RESTRICTIONS 24
      MISSIONS, GOALS, AND OBJECTIVES OF THE SCHOOL
         AND/OR DISTRICT 25
   SUMMARY 29
   FOLLOW-UP ACTIVITIES 30
   REFERENCES 31
   SUGGESTED READINGS 32

2 DETERMINING NEEDS, BUDGETS, AND THE ALLOCATION OF
   FINANCIAL RESOURCES 35
   ASSESSING CONDITIONS, DETERMINING
      NEEDS, AND IDENTIFYING RESOURCES 36

INCORPORATING FINANCIAL RESOURCE NEEDS
    INTO THE SCHOOL IMPROVEMENT PLAN 45
SUMMARY 64
FOLLOW-UP ACTIVITIES 68
REFERENCES 69
SUGGESTED READINGS 69

3 MANAGING AND CONTROLLING THE USE OF FINANCIAL
   RESOURCES 71
   MANAGING FINANCIAL RESOURCES 73
      THE SCHOOL BUDGET 73
      THE BUDGET CALENDAR 74
      THE SCHOOL IMPROVEMENT PLAN AND BUDGET
        DEVELOPMENT 75
   MONITORING THE USE OF FINANCIAL RESOURCES 80
      PROCEDURES FOR MONITORING 80
      BUDGET CODIFICATION 82
      EVALUATING THE MANAGEMENT OF
        FINANCIAL RESOURCES 85
      EVALUATION OF FINANCIAL RESOURCE UTILIZATION 85
   SUMMARY 88
   FOLLOW-UP ACTIVITIES 90
   REFERENCES 91
   SUGGESTED READINGS 91

4 THE ALLOCATION OF HUMAN RESOURCES: STAFFING FOR
   EDUCATIONAL PURPOSES 93
   STAFFING THE SCHOOL FOR EDUCATIONAL PURPOSES 94
      HUMAN RESOURCES PLANNING 94
      AN OPERATIONAL PROCEDURAL MODEL FOR
        PLANNING 95
      FORECASTING PERSONNEL NEEDS 96
      POSITION ANALYSIS AND POSITION DESCRIPTIONS 99
      CONTENTS OF A POSITION ANALYSIS 99
   RECRUITMENT OF HUMAN RESOURCES 106
      AN OPERATIONAL MODEL FOR THE
        RECRUITMENT PROCESS 107

THE EMPLOYMENT APPLICATION—DATA GATHERING
DURING THE RECRUITMENT PROCESS 111
PROFESSIONAL PHILOSOPHY AND PERSONAL
DEVELOPMENT INFORMATION 111
THE RECRUITMENT INTERVIEW 114
THE EVALUATION OF APPLICANTS—
PAPER SCREENING 114
SELECTION OF PERSONNEL 117
OPERATIONS MODEL FOR PERSONNEL SELECTION 117
THE INTERVIEW 121
THE BEHAVIORAL INTERVIEW 122
TALENT ATTRACTION AND SELECTION
SYSTEM INTERVIEW 122
VIDEOTAPED INTERVIEWS 124
THE GROUP INTERVIEW 124
THE STRUCTURED INTERVIEW 125
THE INTERVIEW REPORT FORM 125
SUMMARY 128
FOLLOW-UP ACTIVITIES 129
REFERENCES 129
SUGGESTED READINGS 130

5 THE ALLOCATION OF HUMAN RESOURCES: EFFECTIVE STAFF
UTILIZATION 131
THE STAFF ORIENTATION PROCESS 132
STAFF ORIENTATION DEFINED 132
PURPOSES OF STAFF ORIENTATION 133
GUIDING PRINCIPLES FOR ORIENTATION PRACTICES 134
ORIENTATION PROCESS OPERATIONAL MODEL 135
PROBLEMS OF BEGINNING TEACHERS 137
THE ASSIGNMENT OF PERSONNEL 140
RESPONSIBILITIES OF THE SCHOOL PRINCIPAL 140
ASSESSMENT OF SCHOOL CLIMATE 146
HOW SCHOOL CLIMATE CAN BE IMPROVED 148
THE PRINCIPAL AT WORK 154
HUMAN RESOURCES ALLOCATION AND
TEACHER LOAD 154

STRATEGIES FOR DETERMINING THE LOAD OF TEACHERS IN
  THE SCHOOL 155
FORMULAS FOR TEACHER LOAD MEASUREMENT............. 155
PLANNING AND ORGANIZING AN EFFECTIVE PROGRAM OF
  STAFF DEVELOPMENT 158
A SUCCESSFUL STAFF DEVELOPMENT PROGRAM 158
TRENDS IN PROFESSIONAL STAFF DEVELOPMENT 160
STAFF DEVELOPMENT OPERATIONAL MODEL 160
SUMMARY 165
FOLLOW-UP ACTIVITIES 167
REFERENCES 168
SUGGESTED READINGS 169

1

FINANCING THE SCHOOL PROGRAM

The job of the building principal is one of the most complex, demanding, yet rewarding positions in American society. The principal today faces declining resources, changing demographics, an increasingly knowledgeable public that demands a greater voice in the operation of the school, calls for reform, and legislative bodies that enact unprecedented legislation impacting on schools. The principal must function in an environment with higher levels of expectations and accountability than ever before and at the same time participate in decision making that includes a greater array of stakeholders than previously experienced by school leaders in our society. Accountability for managing the resources of the school rests with the principal and the expectation is high that the decisions related to the allocation of those resources will be shared with the stakeholders of the school.

Every organization operates with human, material, financial, and time resources, and schools are no exception. The extent to which those resources are appropriately allocated, effectively managed, closely monitored, and their use accurately evaluated largely determines the overall success of the school and the principal. Hoyle, English, and Steffy (1990) reported that to change schools and unlock their potential, principals must think differently about resources because the manner in which resources are allocated must reflect the articulated purposes of the school.

1

The decade of the nineties has seen a major shift in the decision-making process and in decision-making responsibility. Whereas for years the principal was seen as the decision maker at the school, the "captain of the ship" and the ultimate authority, the nineties has witnessed a move from a centralized to a decentralized process; decisions are being made at the level closest to their implementation by those who have a vested interest in the results of those decisions. Site-based shared decision making by school improvement teams, site councils, and quality circle groups has witnessed a corresponding shift in the overall approach to school administration, school leadership, and school management. The educational leader, who has a clearly defined personal philosophy and belief system relative to school administration and who has the knowledge, skills, and abilities needed for effective group processes, most likely will be the school administrator who stands the greatest chance for success in the years to come.

Chapter 1 addresses the need for the administrator to develop a personal philosophy and basic beliefs about the decision-making process, collaborative planning, and the allocation of fiscal resources. The resources available to the principal are clearly defined with a suggested framework for conceptualizing the source, function, and use of fiscal resources. Internal as well as external forces that impact upon the utilization of resources in the school are introduced and discussed. Finally, specific models are provided that the school leader can use to: (1) summarize information about financial resources, and (2) discuss school funding and financial resource allocation with school staff, school planning teams, parents, and community members.

Today's school leader must recognize the importance of achieving the maximum benefit from the resources received and used by the school. The time has long since passed when there is "more where that came from." Rather, the demand for greater accountability for the use of public funds is sharply increasing. As reported in *School Business Affairs*, the 1995 Phi Delta Kappa/ Gallup poll of public attitudes toward public schools revealed that lack of proper financial support continued to rank as one of the top concerns, but appearing for the first time was "management of funds/programs" (1995, p. 56). At the same time, there is a corresponding demand to shift the burden of taxation from those who perceive they are paying more than their fair share or to lighten the tax load on the various taxpayer groups. The public as well as legislative and congressional officials have become increasingly concerned about the performance of students in schools, and their willingness to provide additional financial resources to the educational enterprise is waning. School leaders can no longer rely on "funding as usual." As noted by Hoyle, English, and Steffy, "Today's reality is that the public schools must stand in line with the other public institutions and plead for their share of the tax revenue. Taxpayers have become more skeptical of the educational establishment and, whether directly or through elected officials, demand clear answers to such questions as: (1) what are you going to do with the money? and (2) what did you do with the money we gave you last year?" (1990, p. 49). Principals must become even more knowledgeable about how schools are funded. School leaders must seek to understand more fully how individuals and groups, who control the financing of public schools, perceive schools and be able to demonstrate with even greater conviction and accuracy: (1) the ways in which the resources entrusted to them have been utilized to their greatest potential, and (2) the need for additional financial resources. Hoyle, English, and Steffy challenged educators with this comment: "Attempting to peer into the next century is, at best, impossible. School leaders, however, cannot ignore the dynamic trends that unfold before their eyes . . . educational leaders at all levels can take the initiative and fight. School leaders can strive to accomplish the following four essential conditions for the successful revitalization and reform of schools: (1) create an equitable allocation of resources, (2) embrace a future-focused school system, (3) utilize the total community, and (4) share a common vision" (p. 272). This challenge continues to reinforce the need for school leaders to understand the economics of school finance and to prepare themselves to take the initiative to obtain the financial resources needed by schools to effectively serve all students.

A Philosophy and Belief System

The decade of the nineties has witnessed a major shift in the decision-making process in public schools. In recent years, an increased public awareness of the notion of empowerment, shared decision making, participatory management, and local involvement in the operation of schools has caused schools across the country to move toward representation from all stakeholder groups who have a vested interest in the success of the school and in the decision-making processes at the school. In fact, legislation has been enacted in many states that has shifted the decision-making process from Central Office staff to the local school and from the building principal to school groups such as site councils, school improvement teams, and school effectiveness teams.

Inherent in the operation of any school is: (1) the acquisition of those bodies of knowledge required of the school administrator to effectively lead a school, (2) the skills and abilities necessary to effectively apply the knowledge, and (3) the periodic acquisition of relevant data and information applicable to the operation and success of the school. Critical to the success of the administrator, the school, and the decision-making groups is: (1) the manner in which the administrator chooses to share the knowledge and information with the stakeholders, (2) the specific knowledge and information the administrator chooses to share with the stakeholders, and (3) the skill and expertise displayed by the administrator in enabling the stakeholder groups to effectively use the knowledge and information to make appropriate decisions for the school.

Every principal must have a vision of the school in which he or she works. That vision will often include expectations concerning: (1) student success, (2) the overall climate or environment of the school, (3) the processes by which decisions are made, and (4) the ways in which the administrator envisions individuals and groups interacting together.

The principal, as school leader, is a primary recipient of information about the school. That information comes from a variety of sources such as the Central Office, the press, the staff, the students, the parents, and other principals or administrators. Such information can be solicited or unsolicited, accurate or inaccurate, favorable or unfavorable, positive or negative, realistic or unrealistic. The principal is perceived as the "one with the information" and particularly the one with the information needed for decision making. When allocating financial resources, the principal typically is the one who is the first to receive basic information. It is the principal who is notified of the total dollar allocation to the school. Often, this is a block allocation that includes the funds necessary to operate the entire school for one year. Those funds can be utilized for such needs as staffing, transportation, food services, maintenance, supplies, furniture, and equipment. It is at this juncture that the principal acts on personal beliefs and philosophy relative to information sharing. The principal may want to conceptualize an information network within the local school community and identify by name the groups represented. Figure 1.1 reveals those groups that have the greatest degree of personal interest and welfare in the overall success of the school. Today's research clearly suggests that it is those groups that should be involved in the decision-making process of the school.

FIGURE 1.1 SCHOOL DATA AND INFORMATION NETWORK

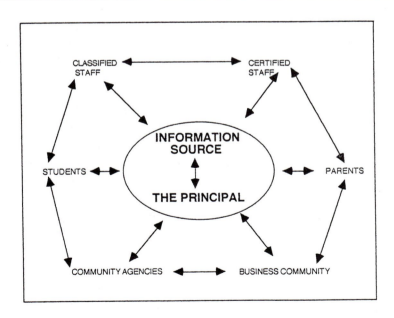

Information sharing typically involves the principal coming to grips with such questions as: (1) what information do I have? (2) what information do I share? (3) how much information do I share? (4) with whom do I share it? and (5) what mechanism will I use to share it? These questions must be answered by the principal in order to work with the immediate staff in planning for the day-to-day and future operations of the school. These questions become even more significant when one considers today's prevailing practice of shared decision making and the widespread involvement of committees or councils or a variety of stakeholder groups. How the principal answers each question and translates those answers into action will send important messages to the staff and to various community groups. For example, principals who choose to involve others in the decision-making process and provide them with all the relevant information will be more likely to create an atmosphere of trust and openness that encourages others to operate in a similar fashion.

Once the principal has developed a conceptual model for data-sharing, the next step is to identify a representative list of individuals, groups, or agencies within each stakeholder group from the entire school community. Figure 1.2 suggests a format the principal might consider when developing the list. As the principal prepares the list, the following occur: (1) it forces the principal to develop a clear picture or perspective of the stakeholder groups that potentially have a genuine interest in the success of the school, (2) it identifies specific individuals and organizations that may become valuable resources to the school, and (3) it provides the school leadership with a core from which to build a communications network for information sharing.

When an atmosphere of trust and openness prevails, fewer "hidden agendas" encroach upon the decision-making process. These kinds of working relationships typically generate a commitment on the part of all participants to make the best decisions possible.

Principals, like all others, bring to the workplace their past experiences, beliefs, and values that impact their decisions and behaviors. The research of the Far West Laboratory for Educational Research and Development reinforced this notion during

FIGURE 1.2 ALL AMERICAN SCHOOL
STAKEHOLDER GROUPS AND REPRESENTATIVES

TYPE OF GROUP	GROUP NAME	REPRESENTATIVE	TELEPHONE NUMBER	ADDRESS
PARENT	ALL AMERICAN PTO			
	BAND BOOSTER			
COMMUNITY SERVICE	ROTARY			
	KIWANIS			
	ALL CITY CHURCH			
COMMUNITY BUSINESS	ABC AUTOMOTIVE			
	HILDA'S HAIR FASHIONS			
	FIRST STATE BANK			
STUDENT GROUPS	STUDENT COUNCIL			
	CLASS/GRADE LEVELS			
CLASSIFIED STAFF GROUPS	OFFICE AND CLERICAL			
	CUSTODIAL AND MAINTENANCE			
CERTIFIED STAFF GROUPS	TEACHER ASSOCIATION			
	DEPARTMENTAL GROUPS			

the time they studied principal behavior and subsequently developed the Peer-Assisted Leadership Program (PAL). An outcome of their research was the creation of their General Framework of Instructional Leadership model. That model clearly demonstrates that the principal's routine behaviors are, in part, a direct result of the principal's beliefs and experiences. Senge (1990) noted that, "over and above self-interest, people truly want to be a part of something larger than themselves. They want to contribute to building something important. And they value doing it with others" (pp. 274–275). The American Association of School Administrators (AASA) noted that "providing teachers with increased involvement in decision making will help meet one of the most important conditions for improving the status and quality of the teaching force in the 1990s and beyond" (1988, p. 29). The principal who agrees with Senge and with AASA will create opportunities for all persons interested in the success of the school to participate in the making of decisions that impact on the operation of the school. An article by Gilchrist (1989) reemphasizes Sharpe's seven common characteristics of good schools and how to attain them. One of the seven characteristics is: "in every effective school, people are informed. Constant communications between administration, staff, parents, and community are a given . . . In any good organization, as demonstrated by the three schools, there is a concern for 'getting the news out.' How this will affect others, and how can I let them know? seems to be the modus operandi" (p. 138).

In their book, *The Wisdom of Teams—Creating the High Performance Organization,* Katzenbach and Smith (1993) wrote that real teams "are a small number of people who are equally committed to a common purpose, goals and working approach for which they hold themselves mutually accountable," (p. 92), and that a high performance team "is a group that meets all the conditions of real teams, and has members who are also deeply committed to one another's personal growth and success" (p. 92). The principal's approach to information sharing, personal philosophy and values will be driven by what is believed about the people in the school and what the leader hopes to create in the form of a collective group of individuals and groups making decisions about the operations and the future of the school.

School leaders must remember that public schools are public institutions and, as such, the public has a right to have access to certain records and information, including financial information. With respect to planning the allocation of the financial and material resources of the school, the leader who shares and discusses available information with the stakeholders in the planning process will create and sustain a much different school climate and atmosphere than the principal who elects to withhold such information.

The principal also brings to the school beliefs about decision making within the school. Glickman (1993) writes that "in the collaborative approach, no hierarchy of authority determines changes. People within the formal hierarchy accept the same rights and responsibilities, vote as others do, and act as others do. Decisions are made through equal distribution of power" (p. 84). He goes on to state that "no group member can hide from the consequences of a decision; whatever has been decided is a group decision, and the entire group is responsible" (p. 84). Leaders who subscribe to this philosophy will provide the opportunity for equal representation and for equal voice in group discussions, deliberations, and decisions.

Figure 1.3 reflects those stakeholders that have the greatest vested interest in the direction, operation, and success of the school. The school leader will be well-advised to include representatives from those groups when setting direction for the school and when allocating financial resources.

The principal serves as a resource person in providing additional information or clarifying information, assists in facilitating group discussion and decision making, and assists in carrying out the wishes and decisions of the group.

Finally, not only will the principal share information with others, but the effective principal will strive for meaningful involvement of stakeholder groups in the decision-making process of the school. The effective leader will be aware of the research on effective schools that indicates that a prevailing characteristic of effective schools is "everyone's continued involvement . . . involvement applies not only to festivals and career exploration; it is a way of doing business. Every decision is made with the input from those to be affected by the decision. The

FIGURE 1.3 STAKEHOLDER GROUPS CONCERNED WITH THE
ALLOCATION OF FINANCIAL RESOURCES

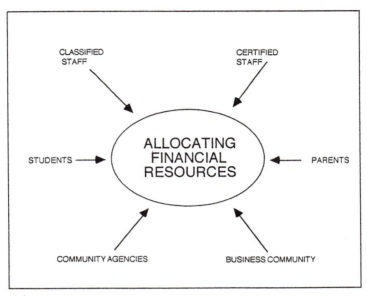

school would not consider operating in isolation. Parents, students, and the community are truly partners in the educational enterprise" (Gilchrist, 1989, p. 137).

RESOURCES AVAILABLE TO THE PRINCIPAL

In the educational enterprise, resources are often referred to as: (1) staffing (human), (2) capital (material), and (3) fund allocations (financial). Financial resources allocated to the school are generally divided into two categories: maintenance and operations, and capital.

School funding formulas and school finance laws are highly complex topics that are rarely fully understood by the public and, in some cases, by educators. Although it is not within the intent or scope of this book to critique or analyze school funding formulae, it is important for the principal to be able to conceptualize the broader scope of school district funding and understand how school funding flows from district funding. For example, school district expenditures typically encompass three major categories: maintenance and operations, capital, and debt service. As is reflected in Figure 1.4, maintenance and operations funding enables the staff to perform the essential and vital functions necessary to the operation of the school. Capital funds enable the school to acquire needed furniture and equipment and/or construct or remodel facilities or campus structures. Debt service funds are used exclusively by the district to repay existing debt incurred by the district. Schools do not accrue this type of debt. The principal who understands these fundamental differences will be able to better comprehend the bigger picture of district and school financing, and also will be able to more clearly articulate to the staff and patrons of the school the specific resources available to the school and how they can be utilized more effectively.

The school administrator also must be aware of the distribution of funds of a typical district. In most educational enterprises, 85% to 90% of fund allocations is needed for maintenance and operations use. Ten percent to 15% of the allocations remain for capital needs and debt service. The typical percentage of expenditures in each category appears in Figure 1.4. This information underscores the importance of the school leader allocating and managing the resources of the school in a manner that will achieve the desired results.

Further examination of how maintenance and operations funds are used in a typical school is reflected in Figure 1.5. One can observe that the major portion of financial resources allocated to the school is committed to salaries and fringe benefits; only 10% of the remaining funds is available for supplies, materials, utilities, and other needs.

Educators, as well as the general public, often are surprised when they learn how school district money is expended. Site councils, school committees, school improvement teams, or other school-level decision-making groups who become involved in varying degrees of resource allocation as a part of the decision-making activities of the school may not be aware of the total amount of funds available for allocation. In most schools, certain fixed charges encumber a very high percentage of funds

FIGURE 1.4 TYPICAL DISTRIBUTION OF FUND EXPENDITURES AT THE DISTRICT LEVEL

AREA OF EXPENDITURE	PERCENTAGE
MAINTENANCE AND OPERATIONS Employee salaries and fringe benefits Supplies: Instructional, office, custodial, etc. Insurance, legal fees Travel, registration fees, meals, lodging	85 %
CAPITAL Classroom furniture and equipment New buildings, remodeling, landscaping Office furniture and equipment Textbooks, audiovisual equipment Library books	6 %
DEBT SERVICE Bond redemption Bond interest	9 %
TOTAL	100 %

FIGURE 1.5 TYPICAL DISTRIBUTION OF MAINTENANCE AND OPERATIONS EXPENDITURES AT THE SCHOOL LEVEL

AREA OF EXPENDITURE	PERCENTAGE OF TOTAL
SALARIES AND EMPLOYEE BENEFITS Salaries OASI Retirement Insurance Workman's compensation Overtime: custodial, secretarial, security, classroom aides	**90 %**
UTILITIES Telephone Electricity Sewer and water Refuse Gas Information services	**4 %**
SUPPLIES Instructional Clerical / office Custodial Lawn / landscaping Library / media Postage	**3 %**
OTHER Contract services Travel: transportation, meals, lodging Conference / workshop registration fees	**3 %**
TOTAL	**100 %**

allocated to the school. For example, salaries and employee benefits draw almost 90% of the school funds, with utilities and other fixed charges taking another 7% of the total allocation. Because the principal typically manages "what the school is allocated" in maintenance, operations, and capital funds, it may be helpful to "visualize" those two major categories of funds and to develop a display of how those funds can be used. Figure 1.6 reflects such a display. As revealed in Figure 1.6, maintenance and operations funds are utilized to purchase services or supplies that tend to be consumed each year. Resources allocated and consumed on an annual basis, such as maintenance and operations funds, require that school leaders carefully analyze the effect of the allocations and the degree to which the utilization of the resources achieve the desired outcomes of the school. On the other hand, capital funds are used for items that have a much longer life expectancy and, consequently, do not require as frequent analysis as do maintenance and operations funds.

TYPES AND SOURCES OF FINANCIAL RESOURCES

It is important for the principal to know the sources of financial resources both available and allocated to the school. First, the source of the funding likely will dictate how the funds can be used. Second, when discussing funding with staff, school groups, parents, or other community groups, it is imperative that the principal has a basic knowledge and understanding of school funding sources. Third, such sources provide a knowledge base that can be used when seeking additional resources for the school.

LOCAL AND NON-LOCAL FUNDS

Funding sources are classified as either *local* or *non-local*. Funds classified as originating from a local source are those funds generated by local (city, county, or state) taxation. Non-local funds are those received from some tax-supported source other than city, county, or state, namely the Federal government. Non-local funds typically are allocated to districts and schools on the basis of a predetermined formula that takes into consideration

FIGURE 1.6 TYPES OF FUNDS ALLOCATED TO THE BUILDING PRINCIPAL AND HOW THEY CAN BE USED

USES OF FUNDS	MAINTENANCE AND OPERATIONS	CAPITAL
CONTRACT SERVICES	XXX	
INSTRUCTIONAL SUPPLIES	XXX	
OFFICE SUPPLIES	XXX	
SALARIES	XXX	
CUSTODIAL SUPPLIES	XXX	
INSTRUCTIONAL AIDS (MEDIA)		XXX
FURNTIURE		XXX
EQUIPMENT		XXX
NEW BUILDINGS		XXX
REMODELING		XXX
VEHICLES		XXX

such factors as the number of individuals in the family and the family's income level. These kinds of funds are entitlement funds and remain available to schools so long as the providing legislation remains in force.

COMPETITIVE GRANTS

Another source of funding is through competitive grants made available by both State and Federal governments. Requests for proposals (RFP's) are made available to districts and/or schools that compete for available funds by submitting proposals that address the specific provisions of the fund. Information about funds available through competitive grants is available in such weekly publications as *Education Funding News* and the *Federal Register Digest Service*. Funds received through competitive grants are usually available for only the duration of the grant or funding period, which in most cases is for one year from the date of the award, but may be as long as three to five years. These monies are typically referred to as "soft" monies because the funding generally ends at the termination of the grant period unless there is legislation renewing the program. In that event, schools or districts are usually asked to reapply.

FOUNDATION FUNDS

Another source of funding is through foundations. Again, foundations and philanthropic organizations have particular types of projects or programs in which they are interested and will provide funds to agencies such as schools or community groups that have programs that enhance or address those interests. As in the case of the competitive grants awarded by the Federal government, funding from foundations and philanthropic organizations is done on an annual basis and is competitive in nature. A good source of information is the *National Directory of Corporate Giving* published by The Foundation Center, New York, New York.

SCHOOL BUSINESS PARTNERSHIPS FUNDS

An increasingly growing source of funding is through school-business partnerships that occur primarily because of the ability of the principal to generate sufficient interest on the part of local businesses to contribute resources to the principal's school. These resources, of course, come in a variety of forms and are generally the result of the principal requesting the specific resource. Frequently, that request results in a cash donation to the school that can be used for the specific purpose outlined in the request. A good example of such a partnership is the organization Operation "QT" Inc., whose specific purpose is to fund after-school programs at schools. Schools that are successful in obtaining funds from the organization typically receive a block grant that can be used as the school chooses with no limitations on how the funds are used other than the program must be some type of after-school program for students.

STUDENT ACTIVITY FUNDS

Another source of funding may be through student activity funds. These are funds generated through student activity programs such as gate receipts from athletic events and fine arts productions, revenue from club sales or projects, or sales through the "infamous Coke machines." Depending on school district policy, all or part of the student activity funds may be available to the building principal for use at the school.

FACILITY RENTAL FUNDS

Another source of revenue for the principal is funds generated through the rental of school buildings or facilities to outside organizations such as churches, local civic organizations, and service clubs. Again, depending on school district policy, all or part of the facility rental funds may be available for use at the school.

As has been noted, there is a variety of sources from which financial resources are received by the school. The school leader may have funds from many, most, or all of the foregoing sources and, as such, will need to know the totality of all that are available in order to ensure effective allocation. Figure 1.7 suggests a visual model that can be used to capture such information and to share it with decision-making constituents in the school. Figure 1.7 could also be used to illustrate the total dollar allocation to the school by simply inserting the dollar amount received in the appropriate cell. For example, the school may have received $1,000,000 from the general tax fund due to rapid student growth within the school's attendance area. Using Figure 1.7 to illustrate the total dollar allocation, the $1,000,000 would be entered in the General Tax/Entitlement cell. If the school received an additional $3,500,000 in local general tax revenue, that figure would be entered in the General Tax/Local cell. Funds received from any other sources would be entered in the appropriate cell, thereby reflecting the sources of all the funds received by the school.

FORCES IMPACTING ON THE ALLOCATION OF FUNDS TO THE SCHOOL

Schools receive financial resources primarily in two different ways. First, the school leader may take the initiative to seek funding other than that provided by the school district. This is accomplished by presenting the needs of students, the school, or the leader's vision of what is to be accomplished with the additional funds. The sources of these kinds of additional funds typically are school/business partnerships, state or federal grants, or private foundations. The second source of funds is those that are provided annually by or through the district. The initial allocation of these funds is predicated primarily on factors such as student enrollment, the socio-economic level of the students attending the school, ethnic and racial balance of the school, desegregation judgments, sudden growth, declining enrollment, special needs students, and perhaps other factors related to student need that are determined to be important by the district, the school, and/or the state. Figure 1.8 represents a conceptual model of those factors. For instance, schools faced with declining student enrollment risk the loss of funds and corresponding loss of staff, programs, or purchasing power of supplies or other needed materials. Conversely, schools experiencing rapid student growth may reap the benefits of increased funding that allows the school to hire additional staff or increase its purchasing power. Schools may also receive additional funds to be used for free and/or reduced lunches as well as for student transportation to and from school if the average annual income

FIGURE 1.7 TYPES AND SOURCES OF FINANCIAL RESOURCES

SOURCE	TYPE			
	ENTITLEMENT	COMPETITIVE	LOCAL	NON-LOCAL
General Tax	XX		XX	
State Grants	XX	XX	XX	
Desegregation	XX		XX	
Federal Grants	XX	XX		XX
Student Activity			XX	
Facility Rental			XX	
Foundations		XX		XX
Partnerships		XX	XX	XX

of families within the school attendance area falls below a certain level.

The allocation of capital funds is based primarily on such factors as the educational program, age of buildings, and student safety. Federal and state grants provide funds that can be used for specific purposes; the principal may have access to those types of funds either because of a successful grant application submitted by the district that awards funds to the schools, or because of a successful grant application submitted by the school. Regardless of the source of funds, the principal typically will have some documentation generated by the Central Office that provides the budget code, a code description, and the total dollar allocation within that code. Information concerning what can be purchased with those funds and information relative to other budget codes to which those funds can be transferred also may

---

FIGURE 1.8 FORCES IMPACTING ON THE ALLOCATION OF FUNDS TO THE SCHOOL

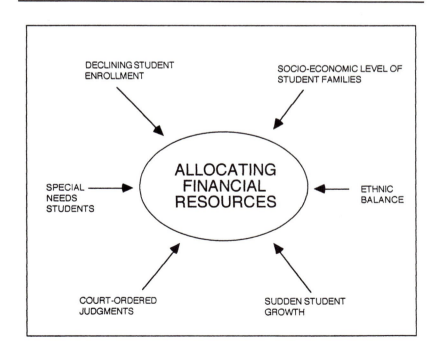

be provided. Summarizing this information into a clear and easily understood format will be beneficial to school administrative personnel as well as to those with whom the information is shared. Consequently, the principal may find it useful to develop a one-page summary sheet that reflects the source of funds, the total amount of the allocation, and the general areas of use of the funds such as is demonstrated in Figure 1.9. Formatting the information in a manner such as this may aid in summarizing the data as well as clarifying the information and presenting a clear and concise picture when discussing the information with other staff members or other stakeholder groups.

FORCES IMPACTING THE UTILIZATION OF FINANCIAL RESOURCES

The degree to which schools have authority to allocate financial resources ranges from complete to perhaps little authority, depending upon the level to which site-based shared decision making has been shifted to the school by the district. Regardless of the degree to which decentralized decision making has been implemented, there are forces that may limit the availability of funds, dictate the areas in which funds may be expended, or may determine the areas in which funds may not be expended. In other words, the source of the funds and the purpose for their allocation often dictate how the funds can be utilized. Several examples of such restrictions are presented in the sections that follow.

FEDERAL AND STATE GRANTS

Federal and state grants are given to schools or districts usually for a specific purpose, such as to improve student achievement in the basic skills or to reduce the instances of drug abuse. These types of grants stipulate the areas in which funds received through the grant can be allocated. For example, a school or a district might have been awarded a competitive grant that provides for additional staff development for teachers. The grant may provide specifically for: (1) hiring of additional staff to coordinate and provide training to teachers, (2) purchasing instructional aids and supplies needed for the training, or (3)

FIGURE 1.9 SUMMARY OF FUNDS ALLOCATED TO ALL AMERICAN SCHOOL

SOURCE	BUDGET CODE	DESCRIPTION	AMOUNT ALLOCATED	USE OF FUNDS				
				STAFF 5300	SUPPLIES 5400	SERVICES 5600	EQUIPMENT 5830	CONSTRUCTION 5820
District	5410	Instructional Supplies	$ 15,000		$ 15,000			
District	5320	Instructional Aides	12,000	12,000				
District	5820	Building Improvements	45,000					$45,000
Federal Grant	5410	Staff Development	2,000		2,000			
Federal Grant	5630	Staff Development	8,000			8,000		
District	5850	Equipment	20,000				20,000	
XYZ Partnership	5810	Computers	10,000				10,000	
TOTAL			$112,000	$12,000	$17,000	$8,000	$30,000	$45,000

purchasing instructional equipment to be used in conjunction with the training. After the funds are received, the staff may see a need to send teachers to an important conference or workshop. However, unless "travel, conference, or workshop" funds were incorporated into the grant proposal, the chances are that travel will not be funded under this grant. This underscores the importance of understanding how funds can be used and planning accordingly.

EMPLOYEE AGREEMENTS OR CONTRACTS

The bargaining agreement between the various employee organizations may dictate that there are certain fixed charges that the school must address before allocating additional resources. For example, the school may be allocated a specific number of teachers based upon a projected number of students, using a negotiated pupil-teacher ratio in a variety of instructional or programmatic situations. Classroom size, the number of laboratory stations, or the number of pieces of instructional equipment may determine the number of students and, in turn, the number of teachers required in a given classroom or program. The fixed charges, then, for those teachers would include salaries and fringe benefits. The funds for those projected expenditures must be encumbered "off the top" before consideration is given to allocating the remaining resources. The school leader must be aware of the specific programmatic and corresponding staffing demands that are mandated by the employee contract or agreement and subsequently determine how much if any salary funds remain that might be used at the discretion of the administrator.

CASE LAW

Case as well as statutory law may dictate how or when a school can use its financial resources. The Fair Labor Standards Act and subsequent case law, for example, have set the standard for non-certificated employees working beyond the customary forty-hour work week. For years, schools employed certificated as well as non-certificated employees to supervise such extra-curricular activities as athletic events, school plays or concerts at a flat rate per hour. Now non-certificated school employees can no longer work beyond the forty-hour work week without being compensated at an overtime rate and receive additional wages for the period worked or be awarded compensatory time off. Of course, this has had a significant impact on the allocation, availability, and utilization of overtime funds. Thus, the school administrator must be aware of the extent to which precedent-setting court cases restrict the ways in which the school can utilize its employees to meet school, student, or programmatic needs with or without some type of compensation.

STATE AND FEDERAL STATUTE

State law may mandate programs at the school, such as a foreign language, instruction in health and sex education, proof of immunization, or a specified number of units required for graduation or promotion. In those instances, school principals have no choice but to provide those programs which, of course, translate into another force impacting the use of financial resources. Federal law also serves as a major force in determining how both district and school financial resources can be used. For example, both public and private organizations are required to make their facilities accessible to the handicapped. Special educational programs for special needs youth have been required for years under what was originally enacted as Public Law 94-142. The Federal School Lunch Program has both nutritional requirements that dictate the types of lunches served to school children as well as regulations that impact on the kinds of products that can be sold on the school campus during times that may be competitive with the school lunch program.

ORGANIZATIONAL RESTRICTIONS

Another force that impacts on how funds are utilized is the restrictions placed on the use of the funds by the organization granting the funds. Specifically, when funds are received by the school from a foundation or philanthropic organization, it generally is after the school or district has submitted a proposal to the organization. The organization typically has established criteria that address a particular program, interest, or need in which it has a particular interest and is willing to assist schools financially that address those programs, interests, or needs. As such, the organization more often than not wants to know how the funds will be spent. Rarely will an organization award a flat grant to a school with no specific plan or purpose for how it will use the funds. The principal may have a more direct influence on the utilization of resources by developing partnerships with local community business and organizations through which funds or services are provided to the school to meet a specific need presented by the school.

Missions, Goals, and Objectives of the School and/or District

As previously noted, planning for the allocation and distribution of funds available to the school principal begins with the mission, goals, and objectives of the school as developed by school personnel and other key stakeholders of the school. The school's mission, goals, and objectives become major forces that impact on the allocation of all the resources available to the school. Administrative personnel must be able to translate the goals and objectives of the school into appropriate resource demands that will enable the school and the staff to accomplish the goals and objectives of the school. This can be accomplished by school leaders working collaboratively with school planning groups to identify specific strategies or interventions needed to accomplish the goals and objectives of the school. In conjunction with those strategies and interventions, related needs in supplies, equipment, materials, and staffing are identified. This kind of information frequently appears in the school's improvement plan.

Figure 1.10 represents a model for a school improvement plan that links the planned strategies and interventions to the resources needed to accomplish the school goals. The principal, using the information suggested in the previous figures, will provide the planning groups with the information regarding the resources allocated to the school. Using the information generated from the school improvement planning process, the groups will identify additional resources needed and compare those amounts with what the school has been allocated. Areas of discrepancy become targeted for obtaining additional resources. The further development of the school improvement plan will be discussed in greater detail in Chapter 2.

FIGURE 1.10 ALL AMERICAN SCHOOL
SCHOOL IMPROVEMENT PLAN: 19__–19__

DISTRICT GOAL: Effective Communications

GOAL DESCRIPTOR: The All American School is a school where there is an interactive communication system that is timely, ongoing, and accurate involving all persons who have a vested interest in the education of its students.

Objectives	Strategies
1. Know stakeholder groups	1. Develop lists of stakeholder groups 2. Develop system of sampling stakeholder groups
2. Determine methods of communication on campus	1. Identify forms of communication, distribution methods, time frames, target audiences, frequency 2. Create separate lists for each group
3. Effective parental communication	1. Develop/implement a parent communication survey 2. Analyze survey results; generate baseline data 3. Develop and implement a corrective plan of action
4. Effective community communication	1. Develop/implement community communication survey 2. Analyze survey results; generate baseline data 3. Develop and implement a corrective plan of action
5. Effective staff communications	1. Develop/implement a staff communication survey 2. Analyze survey results; generate baseline data 3. Develop and implement a corrective plan of action
6. To be determined after survey results are analyzed	Additional strategies to be determined after survey results are tabulated and analyzed
7. To be determined after survey results are analyzed	Additional strategies to be determined after survey results are tabulated and analyzed
8. To be determined after survey results are analyzed	Additional strategies to be determined after survey results are tabulated and analyzed

DOCUMENTED EVIDENCE OF ACHIEVEMENT: This goal will be achieved when 90 percent of the stakeholders surveyed perceive that communication is effective.

GOAL ADMINISTRATORS: Principal, School Improvement Team (SIT) Chair

Persons Responsible	Targeted Beginning Date	Estimated Completion Date	Projected Budget Need	Projected Budget Allocation	Projected Budget Shortfall
1. Principal 2. SIT Chair	1. Month / Year 2. Month / Year	1. Month / Year 2. Month / Year	$ 0	$ 0	$ 0
1. SIT Team 2. SIT Team	1. Month / Year 2. Month / Year	1. Month / Year 2. Month / Year	$ 0	$ 0	$ 0
1. District 2. District 3. SIT Team	1. Month / Year 2. Month / Year 3. Month / Year	1. Month / Year 2. Month / Year 3. Month / Year	$ 500	$ 500	$ 0
1. District 2. District 3. SIT Team	1. Month / Year 2. Month / Year 3. Month / Year	1. Month / Year 2. Month / Year 3. Month / Year	$ 500	$ 300	$ 200
1. District 2. District 3. SIT Team	1. Month / Year 2. Month / Year 3. Month / Year	1. Month / Year 2. Month / Year 3. Month / Year	$ 200	$ 0	$ 200

The effective principal must be knowledgeable of the many forces that influence how funds allocated to the school are expended. Further, in order to ensure that the funds are appropriated into those areas permitted by the various rules, regulations, or policies, the educational leader should develop a system or model that will provide a picture of where and how the financial resources can be used in order to accomplish the goals and objectives of the school. Figure 1.11 suggests a model that the principal might use to conceptualize the forces that impact on the utilization of funds. The model can be useful in clarifying the principal's own thinking about funding allocations and, at the same time, be a useful tool when discussing financial resource allocation and utilization with staff and other constituencies. For example, when the school leader is discussing the allocation of school funds, this model can be used as a point of

FIGURE 1.11 FORCES IMPACTING ON THE UTILIZATION OF SCHOOL FUNDS

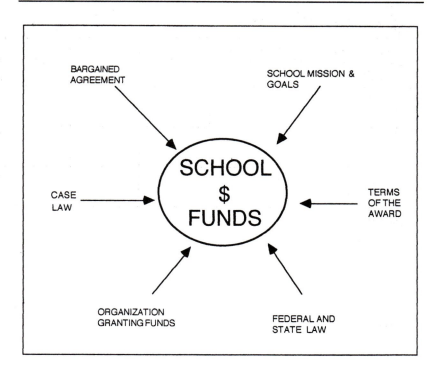

departure to illustrate how allocating funds must be in compliance with the limitations inherent in the law, contract language, or purpose for which the contributing agency is offering the funds to the school. This will be particularly valuable to non-school personnel who are typically unfamiliar with these kinds of restrictions.

SUMMARY

Financing the school program begins with the building principal's personal philosophy and belief system relative to the role in which the key decision makers, the principal stakeholders of the school, are involved in the decision-making process. The school climate, level of collegiality among staff members, degree of commitment to achieve the goals and objectives of the school, and the desire of the entire staff to meet the needs of the children of their school will depend largely upon the leadership of the school principal and the belief system that the principal brings to the workplace. The principal is viewed by many as "the person with the information." The principal who shares the information with those in the decision-making process will be the principal that achieves a learning, collegial, and effective community.

The types and sources of financial resources are of critical importance. School leaders must be cognizant of the fact that financial resources originate with local and state governments, the Federal government, private foundations, philanthropic organizations, and the local business community. In the planning and preparation stages of financial resource allocation, it is also paramount that administrators be aware of the types of funds, maintenance and operations, capital, or other special use, allocated to the school.

When discussing how those resources can be best utilized at the school site, it is imperative to know what limitations are placed on the use of the funds and, conversely, what possibilities exist for the creative usage of the funds. It is incumbent that the principal carefully analyze both limitations and possibilities with each source of financial assistance.

Because states, school districts, and schools differ in many aspects of school finance and in their particular goals and objectives, the principal must carefully analyze the financial resources available to the school, their source and purpose, and the areas in which they can be used in light of the local situation. It is of paramount importance that the school leadership become familiar with statutory limitations or mandates, district policies or procedures, and the language of any Federal grants or organizational awards impacting on the utilization of financial resources. Developing an organized system for summarizing these kinds of information will be most helpful and time-saving.

FOLLOW-UP ACTIVITIES

1. Write a position paper that articulates your personal philosophy and beliefs about decision making and collaborative planning. Describe how these will influence your approach to the distribution or allocation of financial resources.

2. Develop a list of all the organizations or groups that have an interest in or will be impacted by the success of your school. For each group, identify the name or names and telephone numbers of key persons who could serve as potential representatives to your school site council. Develop a plan that would enable you to obtain their commitment to and participation in your vision of an ideal site council operation.

3. Obtain a copy of your school district's budget. Make a list of all the sources of funds that accrue to your district. Using your school budget, make a list of all the sources of funds that have been allocated to your school. Note those sources where funds have been allocated to the district but not to your school, and determine permissible expenditure categories utilizing those funds. Use this information as potential sources for increased allocations in the future.

4. Select a time period of your choice (quarter, semester, year) and review publications such as the *Education Funding News* or the *Federal Register* to determine possible requests for proposals that address existing or anticipated needs at your school. Consult with the person in your district responsible

for grant writing or for monitoring non-local funding and volunteer to develop and submit a proposal seeking the funding.

5. Develop a list of all the businesses in your school's attendance area or in your city. Obtain the name, telephone number, and address of the key contact person in each business that you would work through to generate a partnership relationship with your school. Survey your staff to determine the kinds of support services, equipment, or assistance they would seek from a business partner. Develop a strategy that would enable you to get your message to the businesses and engage their support.

REFERENCES

American Association of School Administrators (1988). *Challenges for School Leaders*. Arlington, VA: Author, p. 29.

Barnett, B. G., Lee, G.V., & Mueller, F. L. *A Manual for Trainers: Peer Assisted Leadership*, Far West Laboratory for Educational Research and Development, Office of Educational Research and Improvement, U.S. Department of Education.

Gilchrist, R. (1989). *Effective Schools: Three Case Studies of Excellence*. Bloomington, IN: National Educational Service, pp. 137–138.

Glickman, C. D. (1993). *Renewing America's Schools*. San Francisco: Jossey-Bass Publishers, p. 84.

Hoyle, J. R., English, F. W., & Steffy, B. E. (1990). *Skills for Successful School Leaders* (2nd ed.). Arlington, VA: American Association of School Administrators, pp. 49–272.

Katzenbach, J.R., & Smith, D. K. (1993). *The Wisdom of Teams*. New York: Harper Business, p. 92.

Phi Delta Kappa (1995). The Big Problems Schools Face: PDK Survey Results. *School Business Affairs*, 61 (10), p. 56.

Senge, P. M. (1990). *The Fifth Discipline: The Art & Practice of the Learning Organization*. New York: Doubleday Currency, pp. 274–275.

SUGGESTED READINGS

Alexander, K., & Salmon, R. (1995). *Public School Finance.* Boston: Allyn & Bacon.

Association for Supervision and Curriculum Development. (1987). *Leadership: Examining the Elusive* (1987 yearbook). Alexandria, VA: Author.

Belasco, J. A. (1991). *Teaching the Elephant to Dance.* New York: Penguin Books USA.

Bennis, W. (1993). *An Invented Life: Reflections on Leadership and Change.* Reading, MA: Addison-Wesley.

Crosby, P. B. (1990). *The Eternally Successful Organization.* New York: Penguin Books USA.

DePree, M. (1989). *Leadership Is an Art.* New York: Dell.

Educational Funding Research Council. (Weekly) *Educational Funding News.* Washington, D.C.

Educational Funding Research Council. (Weekly) *Federal Register Digest Service.* Washington, D.C.

Haile, S. W., editor. (1991). *National Directory of Corporate Giving,* 2nd Edition. New York: The Foundation Center.

Kotter, J. P. (1990). *A Force for Change: How Leadership Differs from Management.* New York: The Free Press, Macmillan, Inc.

Lakein, A. (1973). *How to Get Control of Your Time and Your Life.* New York: Signet.

Lynch, D., & Kordis, P. L. (1988). *Strategy of the Dolphin.* New York: Fawcett Columbine.

Naisbitt, J., & Aburdene, P. (1985). *Re-inventing the Corporation.* New York: Warner Books.

Ouchi, W. G. (1981). *Theory Z.* New York: Avon Books.

Pascale, R. T., & Athos, A. G. (1981). *The Art of Japanese Management: Applications for American Executives.* New York: Warner Books.

Peters, T. J., & Waterman, R. H. Jr. (1982). *In Search of Excellence.* New York: Harper and Row.

Peters, T. J., & Austin, N. (1985). *A Passion for Excellence: The Leadership Difference.* New York: Random House.

Peters, T. (1987). *Thriving on Chaos.* New York: Alfred A. Knopf.

Sergiovanni, T. J. (1991). *The Principalship: A Reflective Practice Perspective* (2nd ed.). Boston: Allyn and Bacon.

U.S. Department of Education. (1991). *Developing Leaders for Restructuring Schools: New Habits of the Mind and Heart.* Washington, D.C.

Walton, M. (1986). *The Deming Management Method.* New York: The Putnam Publishing Company .

Wheatley, M. J. (1992). *Leadership and the New Science: Learning about Organization from an Orderly Universe.* San Francisco: Berrett-Koehler Publishers.

2

DETERMINING NEEDS, BUDGETS, AND THE ALLOCATION OF FINANCIAL RESOURCES

Meeting the needs of a school and the students it serves requires the acquisition, allocation, and effective management of adequate financial resources. The acquisition, allocation, and management of financial resources are truly complex and important tasks of the school leader. In the book *Principals for Our Changing Schools* (1990), four major performance domains for principals are identified, one of which consists of programmatic domains. Programmatic domains focus on the scope and framework of the educational program. They reflect the core technology of schools, instruction, and the related supporting services, developmental activities, and resource base. "Resource allocation consists of planning and developing the budget with appropriate staff; seeking, allocating, and adjusting fiscal, human, and material resources; utilizing the physical plant; monitoring resource use and reporting results" (National Commission for the Principalship, 1990, p. 24). Seeking, allocating, adjusting, and monitoring the use of fiscal resources for an organization as complex as a public school are predicated upon a careful analysis of the needs, goals, and objectives of the school. This is most effectively accomplished through the active engagement of the school staff and representatives from the school community. This group is often referred to as the school planning team.

Schools today face major challenges regarding the availability of resources. In addition to all of the other agencies, programs, or services supported by public funds, one of the more recent challenges facing public school leaders is the notion of choice. A prevailing feeling among policy makers is that competition will force individual schools to respond to the interests of parents and they must either improve or close their doors. Charter schools have become schools of choice and competition. Funds for charter schools are increasing. At the same time, it is becoming increasingly difficult for public schools to maintain existing funding levels and even more difficult to obtain new or additional funds. With financial resources for education becoming more scarce, it is incumbent upon educational leaders at all levels to demonstrate prudent and effective use of financial resources in the operation of their educational enterprises. Chapter 2 addresses maximizing the utilization of financial resources. The chapter discusses ways to utilize data to assess the overall conditions and needs of the school, to determine the needs of the students, to develop a school improvement plan based upon school and student needs, and to allocate financial resources.

ASSESSING CONDITIONS, DETERMINING NEEDS, AND IDENTIFYING RESOURCES

Effective school leaders assume leadership roles in gathering the data and cooperating with staff and community to assess the existing conditions of the school in a variety of areas. As noted in the NAESP publication *Principals for 21st Century Schools* (1990), "A clear distinction in the ability to gather appropriate data for decision making exists between principals who are effective and those who are not. Much of the difference between the two results from the failure of less effective principals to move beyond current assumptions and explore each situation as though it were occurring for the first time. Thus professional judgment gets flawed, because of an incomplete or erroneous data base" (p. 36). *Conditions* include those in such areas as: the physical plant; the curriculum; student demographics; the skill, knowledge, and expertise of staff; levels of student performance and achievement; as well as student participation in extra-curricular activities. The school planning team in cooperation with the building principal analyzes the existing conditions as reflected by the data, identifies specific areas of concern, sets priorities, and projects the financial resources needed to satisfy the concerns. During this assessment and evaluation phase, consideration is given to such areas as:

♦ the overall condition of the school plant

♦ instructional furniture and equipment

♦ plant operational equipment

♦ the changing nature of the student population

♦ the academic performance and behavior of students

♦ the knowledge, skills, and abilities of current staff members

♦ curricular and programmatic needs

♦ the corresponding staffing needs

The assessment and evaluation process requires the collection and analysis of data such as those data pertaining to the academic performance of students, the behavioral tendencies and characteristics of the students, the extra-curricular interests of students, and the demographic composition of the student body. Figure 2.1 reflects a grouping of these kinds of data into five categories: indirect influences on student performance, student descriptors, student cognitive performance, student behavioral performance, and direct influences on student performance. Each cell in the table associated with each major category represents an area in which data are collected, analyzed, and used to project needs which may ultimately translate into a need for new financial resources, additional financial resources, continued financial resources or perhaps even a reduction in financial resources.

If the school planning team needs to know how well the students are performing academically, for example, it would obtain and analyze data such as those reflected in Figure 2.1, column three: Student Cognitive Performance. Student assessment measures—such as criterion referenced test scores, norm referenced test scores, student grades, teacher developed test scores and/or district-developed test scores—provide the school planning team with a variety of data. If student behavior in non-academic areas were of interest to the team, then it would obtain and analyze data such as those reflected in column four in Figure 2.1: Student Behavioral Performance. Throughout the analyses of the data, the practitioner would find that data from a number of cells may be examined, compared, and effectively used to determine needs, to project trends or future programmatic requirements, and to ultimately obtain and allocate financial resources.

For example, if data in student enrollment trends reflected a steady increase in technology-based courses, this information would alert the school staff to monitor the availability of classrooms equipped with the technology required to satisfy the increasing student need and interest in technology-based programs. Using the data to project continued trends, the staff may determine that at a future date it will have to acquire additional funds or re-allocate existing funds in order to meet the changing programmatic needs. Another scenario might suggest that students who are from a particular ethnic background may be receiving lower grades in mathematics, scoring lower in mathematics on nationally norm-referenced tests, scoring lower on teacher or district-made tests, and have a higher absentee rate in comparison to students in comparable grade levels, at the same school, or in other schools in the district or around the state. Such evidence would clearly indicate a need for change in order to enable those students to improve their academic performance in mathematics. Implementing those changes could very well necessitate additional financial resources.

As Figure 2.1 suggests, the principal has access to a wide array of data that can be displayed in an equally wide variety of formats. A primary objective of the principal is to obtain a sufficient amount of data that enable the school planners to make informed decisions about all aspects of school operations. It is equally important to obtain those data in usable, understandable formats. To illustrate one way in which information about grades could be formatted, Figure 2.2 presents the distribution

FIGURE 2.1. ALL AMERICAN SCHOOL ENVIRONMENTAL SCAN

INDIRECT INFLUENCES ON STUDENT PERFORMANCE	STUDENT DESCRIPTORS	STUDENT COGNITIVE PERFORMANCE	STUDENT BEHAVIORAL PERFORMANCE	DIRECT INFLUENCES ON STUDENT PERFORMANCE
COMMUNITY DEMOGRAPHICS	GENDER	CRITERION-REFERENCE TESTS	GRADUATION / PROMOTION RATES	INSTRUCTIONAL DELIVERY SYSTEMS
NUMBER AND TYPES OF COMMUNITY AGENCIES	STUDENT PERCEPTIONS OF SCHOOL	NORM-REFERENCED TESTS	DISCIPLINE REFERRALS	STUDENT SCHEDULING PATTERNS
FAMILY CHARACTERISTICS	ETHNICITY	GRADES	ATTENDANCE / ABSENTEE RATES	INTERVENTION STRATEGIES
COMMUNITY CRIME RATE	GRADE LEVEL ENROLLMENT	STUDENT PORTFOLIOS	PREGNANCIES	USE OF TECHNOLOGY
YOUTH ORIENTED COMMUNITY PROGRAMS	STAFF PERCEPTIONS OF SCHOOL	TEACHER ANECDOTAL RECORDS	EXTRA-CURRICULAR PARTICIPATION	GENERAL PURPOSE CLASSROOMS
COMMUNITY EMPLOYMENT PROFILE	COMMUNITY PERCEPTIONS OF SCHOOL	TEACHER - DEVELOPED TESTS	STUDENT SUSPENSIONS	SPECIALIZED LEARNING LABS
	COURSE ENROLLMENT PATTERNS / TRENDS	DISTRICT-WIDE CONTENT AREA TESTS	DROPOUT RATE	SCHOOL ORGANIZATIONAL PATTERNS
	LIMITED ENGLISH SPEAKING STUDENTS			MANDATED PROGRAMS

of grades by department. Information such as that found in Figure 2.2 could be used to justify a need for financial resources. For example, if the school had made an overt commitment to enable "all students to succeed" and had agreed to provide additional support to every area in which students were not experiencing success, then the departments with the highest percentage of failures would be targeted for increased support. That support could be in the form of additional financial resources to provide such things as additional instructional supplies, increased staff development in new strategies of instructional delivery, or additional staffing. Also, the data in Figure 2.2 might be compared or combined with data from other student performance measures to obtain a more global perspective of student performance before any final decisions were made relative to the allocation of resources.

The analysis of data provides the school leader and the school decision makers with a number of important pieces of information. First, if longitudinal data are being kept and analyzed, these data will reflect student performance levels, perceptions, or conditions from the point at which the data were collected to the present time. Second, the data provide the school with the current status or conditions in all those areas; the school planning team would be able to plot trends. Third, the data give the school a basis upon which to predict trends and identify future needs in all those areas where the school has kept longitudinal data.

Conducting the environmental scan with the corresponding analyses of the data leads the school toward the development of statements that summarize the major findings or conclusions. Many educational leaders have found this to be an extremely worthwhile step toward identifying school needs and developing corresponding goals and objectives. This one- to two-page paper is commonly referred to as the school profile and consists of factual descriptor statements that describe such aspects of the school as the student population, student academic achievement, the educational program, and any other relevant or significant descriptor about the students or the school. The school profile is a valuable tool that can be used by the school leader to inform the school and the community about a number of aspects of the school, such as the educational program, the characteristics of

FIGURE 2.2 ALL AMERICAN SCHOOL
DEPARTMENTAL GRADE DISTRIBUTION
AUGUST 1, 19__, THROUGH JULY 30, 19__

DEPARTMENT	Number of A's	Number of B's	Number of C's	Number of D's	Number of F's	TOTAL GRADES	% age F's
Art	22	7	7	0	2	38	0.5 %
Business	10	16	23	8	6	63	10.0
English	37	89	113	62	40	341	11.7
Foreign Language	10	6	3	0	1	20	5.0
Driver/Safety Education	10	18	9	1	3	41	7.3
Health	10	36	54	18	14	132	10.6
Home Economics	20	43	73	22	4	162	2.5
Mathematics	17	35	63	39	33	187	17.6
Science	28	43	126	43	58	298	19.5
Physical Education	46	7	0	0	1	54	1.9
Psychology	1	3	4	1	2	11	18.2
Social Studies	52	127	156	49	46	430	10.7
Music	76	42	5	0	0	123	0.0
Independent Study	19	3	2	0	0	24	0.0
TOTAL	358	475	638	243	210	1924	
% OF TOTAL	19%	24%	33%	13%	11%		11%

the students served by the school, the curricular and co-curricular areas of interest of the students, and the levels of student performance in a variety of academic programs. Figure 2.3 is an example of a school profile document that contains specific information about student perceptions that would be obtained in a student survey, information about student performance on norm referenced tests, specific information that would have come from the school's student behavioral files, and some information about student demographics. Even this abbreviated sample of a school profile gives the reader some general notion about student academic performance and the ethnic composition of the student body.

Equipped with the conclusions drawn from the data analysis, as well as the school profile statement, the school leader, working closely with representatives on the school planning team from the school and the community, identifies needs and establishes priorities. In order to accomplish these tasks, the following question may be asked: "Based upon the analysis of the data, in what areas of the school or aspects of the school operation (e.g., student achievement, physical facilities, technology, curriculum, staff development) are the gaps the greatest between what is and what we would like to achieve?" As the team works toward arriving at the answer to the foregoing question for each critical area, priorities are established in those areas where the gap between what is and what the staff and the community would like to achieve is the greatest. For example, when analyzing student academic achievement, the school utilizes a variety of assessment tools or measures. Figure 2.4 reflects how those performance assessments could be displayed. The column labeled "Actual" reflects the current performance levels while the column labeled "Desired" reflects the desired performance levels. The third column labeled "Gap" indicates the difference between the current performance level and the expected performance level. The areas where the gaps are the greatest are those areas the staff must consider when identifying priorities for the subsequent school year. Those priorities would have a direct influence upon the acquisition and allocation of funds.

FIGURE 2.3 SCHOOL PROFILE

This document presents summary descriptor statements gleaned from an analysis of a variety of data about our school and the students who attend the school. Data included are the results of surveys of parents, students, staff, and the community as well as performance assessments and measures of a variety of student behaviors.

Student Perceptions

1. 65% of seniors indicated they had attended their high school for 4 or more years.

2. 47% of all students indicated that their high school was as safe as most other campuses.

3. 65% of all students do not work. 31 % of all students work part-time; 4 % work full-time.

4. 29% of all students have thought about dropping out of school during their high school career.

Student Achievement

1. Students taking the SAT scored 93 points below the national average in verbal skills.

2. Students taking the SAT scored 50 points below the national average in mathematics.

3. Students taking the ACT scored 1.6 points below the national average in the composite score.

4. Students taking the ACT scored 1.6 points below the national average in mathematics.

5. Students taking the ACT scored 1.5 points below the national average in English.

6. 34% of the students have a documented reading deficiency.

Student Non-Academic Performance

1. The student absentee rate during the first 100 days was 8.4%.

2. The student dropout rate during the past school year was 14.6%.

3. The student graduation rate during the past school year was 85.4%.

4. 35.6% of the students had excessive absences during the past year.

5. 51.6% of the students come from low income families.

6. 41.4% of the eighth grade students have 3 or more at-risk factors.

Student Demographics

1. 52.2% of the students are Anglo; 29.5% Hispanic; 10.3% Black; 4.3% Asian; 3.7% Native American.

2. Sophomore students have the highest dropout rate.

3. Hispanic students have the highest dropout rate.

FIGURE 2.4 ALL AMERICAN SCHOOL
CRITICAL AREA PERFORMANCE/STATUS GAP ANALYSIS

AREA	ACTUAL	DESIRED	GAP
Student Cognitive Performance			
Standardized Assessments			
ACT Scores (Composite)	19.0	21.0	2.0
SAT Scores (Composite)	881	902	21.0
District Tests: Grade 10			
English (Grade Equivalent)	10.1	10.8	.7
Mathematics (Grade Equivalent)	9.4	10.8	1.4
Science (Grade Equivalent)	9.8	10.8	1.0
Grades: Percentage of Failures			
English	11.7 %	0.0 %	11.7 %
Social Studies	10.7 %	0.0 %	10.7 %
Mathematics	17.6 %	0.0 %	17.6 %
Attendance/Graduation/Dropout Rates			
Attendance	91.6 %	95.0 %	3.4 %
Graduation	85.4 %	95.0 %	9.6 %
Dropout	14.6 %	5.0 %	9.6 %
Physical Plant Facilities & Equipment			
General Purpose Classrooms	26	28	2
Technology Labs	2	4	2
Computers (Student)	36	72	36
Computers (Teachers)	12	28	16

INCORPORATING FINANCIAL RESOURCE NEEDS INTO THE SCHOOL IMPROVEMENT PLAN

Up to this point, the school leader has shared and discussed information and data with the school staff and representatives from the community. Representative groups have examined the data, analyzed the data, and drawn conclusions. A school profile has been developed that describes the school and the student population in brief factual statements that enable anyone reading the document to formulate an overall perspective of the school. Trends have been projected that alert the school to areas that will need attention in the future. The data analyses have shown where gaps exist between current performance or conditions and desired performance or conditions.

The effective school leader utilizes this information and, with the school planning team, identifies the specific goals for the school for the next one-, two-, or three-year period. Throughout the goal-development stage, input is aggressively sought from those persons responsible for achieving the goals. All teachers, staff members, and departments have an opportunity to provide input into the development of the goals and have an opportunity to design the action plan needed to achieve the goals. These goals become the targets toward which the school directs its efforts and allocates its financial resources.

Glickman (1993) poses two questions for the school planning team: "With our existing money, are we doing the right thing? With more money, would we be doing more of the right things?" (p. 74). Certainly, as the school begins to develop goals and objectives, the staff will more likely be doing more of the right things related to the allocation of financial resources.

The effective school leader provides the staff with a planning tool that can be used to develop objectives and strategies designed to achieve the school goals. Figure 2.5 is a sample worksheet that can be used as an effective planning tool. School leaders such as department chairs, grade level chairs, special function chairs, teachers, or the maintenance supervisor, for example, might be asked to complete the worksheet. The format enables the user to link a number of components of a comprehensive school improvement plan. For example, at the top of

FIGURE 2.5 ALL AMERICAN SCHOOL
SCHOOL IMPROVEMENT PLAN: 19__–19__

SCHOOL GOAL. Students will improve their performance in reading.

DOCUMENTED EVIDENCE OF ACHIEVEMENT: The number of students with a documented reading deficiency will be reduced by 10%.

Objectives	Strategies
1. Students will increase mastery of the essential skills in reading.	1. Teachers will use graphic organizers: KWL (What do you **know**? What do you **want** to know? What did you **learn**?) and mapping.
	2. Teachers will record student performance with the use of reading logs.
	3. Teachers will implement reading for pleasure activities.
	4. Teachers will implement reading for information activities.
	5. Teachers will use six journalistic questions across the curriculum.
	6. Teachers will implement the SQ3R (Survey, Question, Read, Recite, Review) program across the curriculum.

GOAL ADMINISTRATORS: Principal, School Improvement Team (SIT) Chair

Persons Responsible	Targeted Beginning Date	Estimated Completion Date	Projected Budget Need	Projected Budget Allocation	Projected Budget Shortfall
Classroom. Teachers	1. Sept, 19__	1. May, 19__	$112.00	$112.00	–
Classroom Teachers	2. Sept, 19__	2. May, 19__	$1,000.00	–	$1,000.00
Classroom Teachers	3. Sept, 19__	3. May, 19__	–	–	–
Classroom Teachers	4. Sept, 19__	4. May, 19__	–	–	–
Classroom Teachers	5. Sept, 19__	5. May, 19__	–	–	–
Classroom Teachers	6. Sept, 19__	6. May, 19__	$150.00	$150.00	–
	Month / Year	Month / Year			
	Month / Year	Month / Year			
	Month / Year	Month / Year			
	Month / Year	Month / Year			
	Month / Year	Month / Year			

the document, the school goal is stated and serves as a reminder of what the stated objectives and related strategies are intended to achieve. The documented evidence of achievement represents the improvement goal that the school has accepted as success. The goal administrators are the individuals charged with the responsibility for the overall accomplishment of the goal. In addition, the document becomes a tool usable by all members of the staff throughout the year. The strategies, timelines, evaluation procedures, persons responsible, budgetary requirements, and staff development needs are all clearly stated and serve as a checklist to monitor activities related to implementation of the strategies. A vital piece of information on the document is the projected budgetary needs identified by the staff that are utilized when the school allocates its financial resources. The document also serves as a tool to measure the effectiveness of the strategies implemented.

The illustration in Figure 2.5 reveals how information found in the school profile impacts on the overall budgetary process. Let us assume that the reading specialists were asked to submit their plan for improving student performance in reading. Figure 2.5 is an example of what the reading specialists might submit. For example, it was noted in Figure 2.3 that 34% of the students have a documented reading deficiency. The school planning team determined that mastering reading was an important component of a student's learning and established the school goal that "Students will improve their performance in reading." (See Figure 2.5, School Goal.) The reading specialists in the school determined that their first objective would be that "Students will increase mastery of the essential skills in reading." They then identified six strategies they would implement and projected related timelines. Most important for the budgeting process, they identified anticipated budgetary needs, predicted the areas and amounts where they expected to receive funds, and projected the area and amount where they predicted receiving no budget funds.

Each individual, division, or department is asked to identify: (1) the specific objectives that must be met in order for the school goals to be achieved, and (2) the specific strategies or action plans that will be designed to achieve the objectives. The individual, division, or department determines the persons responsible for implementation, the timelines, and, most important, the projected costs of implementation. As each individual plan emerges, consideration must be given to the areas of potential need such as: instructional supplies, instructional equipment, staffing, textbooks, in-service education, new or remodeled facilities, and scheduling. The individual, division, or department prepares a worksheet similar to that shown in Figure 2.5 for each school-wide goal.

The next step is to summarize all the financial needs incorporated in the departmental plan. Each department or division will be expected to describe briefly the new program or proposal identified in the school improvement plan and the costs related to the proposal. Using the reading specialists as an example, Figure 2.6 reflects the information provided by the reading specialists. Departments may have two, three, or four new programs or strategies incorporated into their school improvement plan. Any new or additional funding required for implementation is entered into the respective columns. A planning sheet of this type enables the divisions or departments to summarize all the new programs and the proposed related costs in the departmental component of the school-wide school improvement plan. Should the principal choose to collect these documents, a succinct summary of the new programs proposed throughout the school and the projected costs is readily available for reference.

The next step in the sequence of preparing information for the presentation of next year's budget is for the department to submit the total departmental budget request. In most districts, there are certain funding encumbrances over which the school has no control. Those areas may include: staffing, utilities, transportation, or specific mandated programs. In addition, districts may use a specific per-pupil allocation to allocate funds for staffing, instructional supplies, or transportation predicated upon student enrollment within the program. Those programs may include: special education, bilingual education, migrant education, or students from lower socio-economic families. In these cases, the school staff usually does not have the authority to transfer funds from one spending code to another. However, there

FIGURE 2.6 READING SPECIALISTS DEPARTMENT
19__/19__ BUDGET /PROPOSAL WORKSHEET

PROGRAM/PROPOSAL	5410 INSTRUCT. SUPPLIES	5412 OFFICE SUPPLIES
The reading specialists will implement a program with all teachers to train students to use reading logs.	$ 800	$ 200
TOTAL	$ 800	$ 200

5600 CONTRACT SERVICES	5640 EQUIPMENT REPAIR	5700 TRAVEL & REGISTRATION FEES	5800 FURNITURE & EQUIPMENT	OTHER	TOTAL
					$ 1,000
					$ 1,000

will be funding areas where schools may specify the amounts they decide to allocate in each category. Figure 2.7 is an example of a worksheet that the principal may provide to the departments to assist in presenting the total budget needs for the upcoming school year. First, Figure 2.7 reflects the current year fund allocation. Second, the department chair or individual teacher is expected to enter the amount of funding needed for the next school year in the appropriate budget areas. The information in Figure 2.7 enables the department to review the current year's financial allocation and plan the utilization of funds for the forthcoming year. Projected budget needs for the next school year are entered both from existing sources as well as from new or additional funding sources. As was noted in Figure 2.5, the reading specialists projected that they would need an additional $1,000 in supplies, and they are requesting that the funds come from new or additional discretionary funding sources, as reflected in Figure 2.7. This information is valuable to the school leader because it presents a clear and succinct summary of the discretionary funding requested by the department.

Every individual, division, and department submits to the principal a worksheet similar to that in Figure 2.6. The principal consolidates the requests from all the divisions or departments into a school-wide request document that is used for discussion purposes by the planning team. After the school staff, divisions, and departments have developed their respective action plans and have determined the related financial needs for the upcoming school year, the principal will reconvene the planning team. At this point, the principal will present to the school planning team the information obtained from the individuals, divisions, and departments reflecting their needs for *additional* financial resources. That document is reflected in Figure 2.8. During the planning team meeting, each division and department discusses its budgetary needs using as a resource the divisional/departmental action plan developed as represented in Figure 2.5, as well as the document summarizing the divisional or departmental needs as reflected in Figure 2.6. Of course, other resource materials may be used, but the two primary documents are those reflected in these examples. This is advantageous to the principal as well as to the members of the planning team, primarily

FIGURE 2.7 BUDGET RECAP/REQUEST WORKSHEET
READING SPECIALISTS DEPARTMENT
19__–19__ SCHOOL YEAR

BUDGET CODE	USE OF FUNDS	CURRENT YEAR ALLOCATIONS	BUDGET REQUEST FOR NEXT YEAR	NET INCREASE / DECREASE IN REQUEST	REQUEST FOR ADDITIONAL DISCRETIONARY FUNDS	NET INCREASE / DECREASE IN REQUEST	TOTAL FUNDS REQUESTED NEXT YEAR
5410	INSTRUCTIONAL SUPPLIES	112	112	–	800	800	912
5412	OFFICE SUPPLIES	150	150	–	200	200	350
5310	TEACHER SALARIES						
5320	INSTRUCTIONAL AIDE SALARIES						
5450	CUSTODIAL SUPPLIES						
5800	FURNITURE / EQUPMENT		5,000	5,000			5,000
5640	EQUIPMENT REPAIR						
5700	TRAVEL & CONFERENCE REGISTRATION FEES	150	150	–			150
5600	CONTRACT SERVICES						
5810	INSTRUCT AIDS / MEDIA						
5820	TEXTBOOKS						
5900	CONSTRUCTION		20,000	20,000			$ 20,000
TOTAL		$ 412	$25,412	$25,000	$ 1,000	$ 1,000	$ 26,412

FIGURE 2.8 ALL AMERICAN SCHOOL
19__/19__ BUDGET PLANNING/PROPOSAL WORKSHEET

PROGRAM / PROPOSAL	5410 INSTRUCT. SUPPLIES	5412 OFFICE SUPPLIES
High School Example	1,500	600
Art Department	2,500	500
Business Department		
Elementary School Example		
Primary Level (K - 3)	1,200	—
Middle Level (4 - 6)	2,400	500
Junior High (7 - 8)	1,650	300
Reading Specialists	**800**	**200**
School-wide contingency (Elementary or High School)	1,000	2,500
TOTAL SCHOOL-WIDE REQUESTS	$ 11,050	$ 4,600

5600 CONTRACT SERVICES	5640 EQUIP. REPAIR	5700 TRAVEL & REGIS. FEES	5800 FURNITURE & EQUIP.	—— OTHER	TOTAL
—	150	100	–	—	$ 2,350
–	1,200	600	–	–	4,800
–	–	75	–	–	1,275
–	–	350	3,000	500	6.750
–	–	400	–	–	2,350
–	–	–	–	–	**1,000**
500	2,500	1,000	–	–	7,500
$ 500	$ 3,850	$ 2,525	$ 3,000	$ 500	$ 26,025

because these tables represent a common format for displaying departmental objectives, strategies, and needs used throughout the entire school. During this discussion, and subsequent discussions if needed, school-wide priorities are reaffirmed, divisional or departmental funding priorities are established, and fund allocations are made.

This is also the time when the principal identifies the sources of funding and the amounts available through each source. The effective principal, at this juncture, is wise to identify the sources of all discretionary funds available to the school, the specific functions to which the funds have either been or could be allocated, and any special programs or projects to which the funds have already been encumbered. Figure 2.8 suggests a format the school leader might use to present that information. Although the information displayed in Figure 2.8 shows examples of how the data might look in a high school or an elementary school, the data in bold type demonstrate how the request from the reading specialists for the additional $1,000 continues to appear in the suggested documents.

Utilizing the information the school leader receives about funding sources, amounts of funding, and permissible uses for the funds, he/she enters the information on the form suggested in Figure 2.9. The school planners now have, for decision-making purposes, the total of all the discretionary funds allocated to the school both by source and by function or usage. Some funds are not discretionary at the school level; their usage is already predetermined by the funding source, state or federal law, or mandate. The funds itemized in Figure 2.9 are those for which the school planning team has authority to disperse among the various divisions within the school.

Up to this point, the school planning team has: (1) listened to and discussed the presentations from every department or division, during which time they presented their action plans, strategies, and financial needs as they relate to the school needs, priorities, and goals (Figures 2.5, 2.6, and 2.7), and (2) analyzed the sources of financial resources, the amounts from each source, and the functions or permissible uses of the funds as prescribed by the source (See Figure 2.9).

Glickman (1988) stated, "For a school to decide what it wants for students is the first step. The second step is to allocate its

FIGURE 2.9 ALL AMERICAN SCHOOL
SUMMARY OF DISCRETIONARY FUNDS AVAILABLE
19__–19__ SCHOOL YEAR

USES OF FUNDS	SOURCE OF FUNDS							
	M & O	CAPITAL	DESEGRE-GATION	FEDERAL GRANT	BUSINESS PARTNER	STATE GRANT	OTHER	TOTAL
5410 INST. SUPPLIES	$15,000			$ 5,000		$ 5,000		$ 25,000
5412 OFFICE SUPPLIES	5,000							5,000
5310 TEACHER SALARIES								
5320 INST. AIDE SALARIES	20,000		10,000		5,000			35,000
5450 CUSTODIAL SUPPLIES	10,000							10,000
5800 FURNITURE / EQUPMENT		50,000	20,000					70,000
5640 EQUIPMENT REPAIR	2,000							2,000
5700 TRAVEL & CONF. REGIS. FEES	15,000		5,000	5,000				25,000
5600 CONTRACT SERVICES	10,000							10,000
5810 INSTRUCT. AIDS / MEDIA	10,000							10,000
5820 TEXTBOOKS	10,000	20,000						30,000
5900 CONSTRUC-TION	50,000	50,000						100,000
TOTAL	$ 147,000	$ 120,000	$ 35,000	$ 10,000	$ 5,000	$ 5,000		$ 322,000

resources accordingly" (p. 74). The school planning team is now ready to allocate the discretionary funds on the basis of: (1) departmental demonstrated need and priority as reflected in the departmental school improvement plan, and (2) the departmental relationship to the school-wide goals, needs, and priorities. A copy of Figure 2.10 is prepared for each division or department and is used by the school planning team to record the allocation of discretionary funds. Using the information presented in Figure 2.9, the planning team allocates funds and enters the amounts allocated in each representative cell on each departmental sheet. Again, the example shown in Figure 2.10 is of the Reading Specialists Department and shows that the $1,000 requested was, in fact, allocated by the school planning team.

Once the final school-wide allocations have been made and Figure 2.10 has been updated for each department with the current information, Figure 2.11 is completed and reflects a summary of the discretionary funds allocated. It is entirely possible that the data in Figure 2.11 will be the same as the data in Figure 2.9, except that the table heading reflects "Allocated" rather than "Available." However, the school may have transferred funds from one usage function to another in those areas where it had that prerogative. If that, in fact, were to happen, then the numbers in those cells affected would be different in Figure 2.11 than they were in Figure 2.9. For example, the school planning team may choose to allocate $2,500 additional funds to code 5410, Instructional Supplies, and chose to allocate $2,500 less to code 5412, Office Supplies. The cell in Figure 2.11, 5410 Instructional Supplies/M & O, would reflect $17,500 and the cell, 5412 Office Supplies/M & O, would reflect $2,500. The school leader now has a packet of information that shows the allocation of discretionary funds at the school. Figure 2.11 contains the total allocation and serves as a cover page. Following the cover page, each division or department has a page similar to Figure 2.10 that contains the specific amount of the allocations by: (1) funding source, and (2) function.

This packet becomes a very useful tool for the school leader when discussing the financial aspects of school operations and serves as a clear and concise reminder of the funds he or she is expected to effectively manage.

FIGURE 2.10 ALLOCATION OF DISCRETIONARY FUNDS
READING SPECIALISTS DEPARTMENT
19__–19__ SCHOOL YEAR

USES OF FUNDS	SOURCE OF FUNDS							
	M & O	CAPITAL	DESEGRE-GATION	FEDERAL GRANT	BUSINESS PARTNER	STATE GRANT	OTHER	TOTAL
5410 INST. SUPPLIES	$ 800							$ 800
5412 OFFICE SUPPLIES	200							200
5310 TEACHER SALARIES								
5320 INST. AIDE SALARIES								
5450 CUSTODIAL SUPPLIES								
5800 FURNITURE / EQUPMENT								
5640 EQUIPMENT REPAIR								
5700 TRAVEL & CONF. REGIS. FEES								
5600 CONTRACT SERVICES								
5810 INSTRUCT. AIDS / MEDIA								
5820 TEXTBOOKS								
5900 CONSTRUC-TION								
TOTAL	$ 1,000							$ 1,000

FIGURE 2.11 ALL AMERICAN SCHOOL
SUMMARY OF DISCRETIONARY FUNDS ALLOCATED
19__–19__ SCHOOL YEAR

USES OF FUNDS	SOURCE OF FUNDS							
	M & O	CAPITAL	DESEGRE-GATION	FEDERAL GRANT	BUSINESS PARTNER	STATE GRANT	OTHER	TOTAL
5410 INST. SUPPLIES	$15,000			$ 5,000		$ 5,000		$ 25,000
5412 OFFICE SUPPLIES	5,000							5,000
5310 TEACHER SALARIES								
5320 INST. AIDE SALARIES	20,000		10,000		5,000			35,000
5450 CUSTODIAL SUPPLIES	10,000							10,000
5800 FURNITURE / EQUIPMENT		50,000	20,000					70,000
5640 EQUIPMENT REPAIR	2,000							2,000
5700 TRAVEL & CONF. REGIS. FEES	15,000		5,000	5,000				25,000
5600 CONTRACT SERVICES	10,000							10,000
5810 INSTRUCT. AIDS / MEDIA	10,000							10,000
5820 TEXTBOOKS	10,000	20,000						30,000
5900 CONSTRUC-TION	50,000	50,000						100,000
TOTAL	$ 147,000	$ 120,000	$ 35,000	$ 10,000	$ 5,000	$ 5,000		$ 322,000

Although the discussion to this point has focused primarily on maintenance and operational funds, school personnel and officials are also charged with the responsibility of identifying furniture and equipment needs, prioritizing their need in the overall school plan, justifying their requests, and planning for their acquisition. Again, data are analyzed to help determine which furniture and equipment need to be replaced or repaired, and which programs need more space (i.e., classrooms or labs) in order to service appropriately a growing student population or to meet effectively changing student needs or performance.

As has been suggested previously, planning documents or worksheets are most helpful to school personnel when surveying existing conditions, when identifying potential needs, and when preparing requests. Figure 2.12 is a document that is used by an individual division or department to reflect existing conditions or status as well as the projected need and corresponding estimated costs. Each division or department would be expected to supply the applicable information in the chart. For example, if a grade level is projected to increase enrollment that would necessitate another classroom in two years, the current number of classrooms would be entered in the Current Number/Classrooms cell and the projected number of classrooms needed entered in the Projected Number Needed Next Year/Classrooms cell. The Gap/Difference/Classroom cell would reflect the difference between current and projected. The estimated cost per classroom would be entered in the Estimated Cost Per Classroom cell providing the grade level chair, school leader, and school planning team with critical information needed for long-term planning and fund allocation.

Assume that the reading specialists are of the opinion that they need a classroom to implement their strategies next year to achieve their objective. They would enter 0 in the Current Number/Classrooms cell and enter 1 in the Projected Number Needed Next Year/Classrooms cell. The net difference would be 1 and entered in the Gap/Difference/Classroom cell. Assume also that they determined that the most expedient way to obtain a new classroom would be to utilize a portable/temporary facility costing approximately $20,000. That amount is entered in the Estimated Total Cost/Classrooms cell. In addition to the classroom,

FIGURE 2.12 READING SPECIALISTS DEPARTMENT FURNITURE/ EQUIPMENT/FACILITIES PLANNING WORKSHEET

STATUS	CLASS-ROOMS	MEDIA CENTER	AUDITORIUM	GYMNASIUM	PLAY-GROUNDS
CURRENT NUMBER	0				
PROJECTED NUMBER NEEDED: NEXT YEAR	1				
GAP / DIFFERENCE	1				
ESTIMATED TOTAL COST	$20,000				
PROJECTED NUMBER NEEDED: FUTURE YEARS					
GAP / DIFFERENCE					
ESTIMATED TOTAL COST					

COMPUTER LABS	SCIENCE LABS	CLASSROOM FURNITURE	CLASSROOM EQUIPMENT	PLAYGROUND EQUIPMENT	TOTAL
	0	0			
	1	25			
	1	25			
	$ 20,000	$ 5,000			$ 25,000

the reading specialists project they will need 25 student stations. They would enter 0 in the Current Number/Classroom Furniture cell and 25 in the Projected Number Needed Next Year/ Classroom Furniture cell. They would also enter 25 in the Gap/ Difference/Classroom Furniture cell. Using the cost per station of $200, they would enter $5,000 in the Estimated Total Cost/ Classroom Furniture cell. Figure 2.12 is an example of how this worksheet would appear with the information provided by the reading specialists.

Following the budget discussions and final budget allocations by the school planning team, each department is supplied with a document reflecting the final budget allocations. A copy of the departmental budget allocations will be kept by the principal and a school-wide file may be given to the school improvement team. Figure 2.13 reflects the total allocation of discretionary funds to the reading specialists and will be used by the specialists to order supplies and services for the next school year. In this example, the specialists were allocated the total amount requested in codes 5410, 5412, and 5700. Funding for the construction of the classroom and for the purchasing of furniture and equipment was not allocated. The information is consolidated from each department into a school-wide document and used for discussion purposes by the school planning team to prioritize needs, to allocate existing capital funds, or to submit requests for additional capital funds.

The school leader may also want each division or department to prepare a Budget Justification Report as reflected in Figure 2.14. The division or department is asked to supply the information to the school planning team and be prepared to discuss the request during the time the school planning team is prioritizing and allocating capital resources.

SUMMARY

In Chapter 2, the discussion has focused upon a step-by-step, orderly process that can be utilized by the effective school leader to assess school-wide conditions in a variety of areas: student academic performance, student behavior, student demographic characteristics, and programmatic offerings. It was suggested that the school leader begin with an environmental scan and a

Figure 2.13 Final Budget Allocation
Reading Specialists Department
19__–19__ School Year

BUDGET CODE	USE OF FUNDS	CURRENT YEAR ALLOCATIONS	BUDGET REQUEST FOR NEXT YEAR	NET INCREASE / DECREASE	REQUEST FOR ADDITIONAL DISCRETIONARY FUNDS	NET INCREASE / DECREASE	TOTAL
5410	INSTRUCTIONAL SUPPLIES	912					912
5412	OFFICE SUPPLIES	350					350
5310	TEACHER SALARIES						
5320	INSTRUCTIONAL AIDE SALARIES						
5450	CUSTODIAL SUPPLIES						
5800	FURNITURE / EQUPMENT						
5640	EQUIPMENT REPAIR						
5700	TRAVEL & CONF REGIS FEES	150					150
5600	CONTRACT SERVICES						
5810	INSTRUCT AIDS / MEDIA						
5820	TEXTBOOKS						
5900	CONSTRUCTION						
TOTAL		$ 1,412					$ 1,412

FIGURE 2.14 BUDGET JUSTIFICATION REPORT

Department_____ Date:_____

Item Requested_____ Budget Code:_____

Please complete this report with the requested information to assist the school planning team by the date cited below.

1. COMPLETE DESCRIPTION OF THE ITEM (Define: What is it?)_____

_____

_____

2. WHAT IS THE ITEM USED FOR AND WHY IS IT NECESSARY?_____

_____

_____

3. WHAT MANUFACTURER IS REQUESTED?_____

4. OTHER ACCEPTABLE BRANDS_____

5. ITEM NUMBER OR STOCK NUMBER_____

6. SPECIFIC CURRICULA / PROGRAM DEPENDENT UPON THIS ITEM?_____

_____

7. OTHER RATIONALE JUSTIFYING THE PURCHASE OF THIS ITEM_____

_____

_____

_____

SIGNATURE_____   _____
       Teacher/Department/Division Chairperson   Principal or Appropriate Administrator

COMMENTS: SCHOOL IMPROVEMENT (PLANNING) TEAM

_____ REQUEST APPROVED   AMOUNT ALLOCATED / APPROVED: $_____

SIGNATURE_____   DATE_____
      School Improvement (Planning) Team Chairperson

wide variety of data sources was identified. The school leader was advised to develop a school profile providing school decision makers with specific factual statements that would enable them to develop an overall perspective of the school, highlight areas of success, and alert them to potential areas of concern. Utilizing the conclusions drawn from the data analysis, it was suggested that the school leader work closely with the school planning team, involve all staff members in the process, and identify specific school-wide goals that address the areas of concern that surface from the analysis of the data.

Specific planning documents and worksheets were presented that enable the school leader to more clearly and concisely present and collect information relative to financial sources, needs, and requirements and to make intelligent decisions based upon accurate information. Three types of documents were presented in Chapter 2. First, the summary documents such as the Environmental Scan, Departmental Grade Distribution, School Profile, Critical Area Performance/Status Gap Analysis will be used readily by the principal and school planning team to gain a perspective of the conditions at the school, of student performance, and of stakeholder perceptions that will guide them in setting school goals and objectives. Second, specific planning documents such as the School Improvement Plan, Budget Planning/Proposal Worksheet, Budget Recap/Request Worksheet, and the Budget Planning/Proposal Worksheet enable the staff to identify financial needs as related to the school improvement plan. Finally, the Summary of Discretionary Funds Available, Allocation of Discretionary Funds, and the Summary of Discretionary Funds Allocated provide the principal and the staff with information about the sources of funds and become the documents reflecting the areas to which funds are allocated.

Utilizing documents such as these enables the school leader to collect and present factual information in clear and understandable terms. The school leader who engages in these kinds of practices and who facilitates decision making based upon factual information in a logical sequential process will more likely find enthusiastic and dedicated support and commitment from the staff and the community.

FOLLOW-UP ACTIVITIES

1. Schedule a meeting with the school maintenance foreman and the district's director of maintenance. Conduct a visual inspection of your entire school plant analyzing the condition of such areas as the roof, painted surfaces, sidewalks, heating and cooling equipment. Ask for a review of and status report on the current maintenance costs and the expected life span of existing equipment and the anticipated replacement needs and costs. Conduct a similar meeting with the cafeteria manager and director of food services to inspect the kitchen equipment in the cafeteria. Prepare a school-wide list of maintenance and capital needs for both areas.

2. Utilizing the student descriptors found in the second column of Figure 2.1 or others important to your situation, gather data and develop a complete profile of the students attending your school.

3. For each student grouping such as gender, ethnicity, or grade level, gather student cognitive performance data from a variety of performance measures. Determine the student group or groups that are performing to the greatest degree below expected performance levels. Likewise, determine the student group or groups that are performing above expected performance levels. Discuss this information in a faculty meeting. Ask the faculty for its reaction, if there are any surprises, or does the information suggest any changes or needs. Prepare a document that summarizes faculty observations relative to the data.

4. Select the student group performing at the greatest level below expected performance level and determine those students' course enrollment patterns. Calculate the total amount of funds allocated to those courses. Ask the following questions: Are the school's instructional supply funds proportionately allocated to those students who are in the greatest need of instructional attention or need? Do staffing allocations such as instructional aides, counselors, or smaller class sizes support the need to provide special assistance to low-

performing students? Determine how this information might be used when allocating financial resources in the future.

5. Prepare a document similar to Figure 2.9 that summarizes all of the discretionary funds allocated to your school during the current school year. Determine which courses, grade levels, or programs to which those funds have been allocated. Prepare, present, and discuss the information with your administrative team, department or grade level chairs, and faculty. Ask for their suggestions relative to other sources of funds and what strategies the school might utilize to obtain those additional or new funds.

REFERENCES

Glickman, C. D. (1993). *Renewing America's Schools*. San Francisco: Jossey-Bass Publishers, p. 74.

National Association of Elementary School Principals (1990). *Principals for 21st Century Schools*. Alexandria, VA: Author, p. 36.

National Commission for the Principalship, (1990). *Principals for Our Changing Schools*. Fairfax, VA: Author, pp. 23–24.

SUGGESTED READINGS

Alexander, K., & Salmon, R. (1995). *Public School Finance*. Boston: Allyn & Bacon.

American Association of School Administrators (1988). *Challenges for School Leaders*. Arlington, VA.: Author.

Hoyle, J.R., English, F. W., & Steffy, B. E. (1990). *Skills for Successful School Leaders*, (2nd ed.). Arlington, VA: American Association of School Administrators.

Jordan, K. F., & Lyons, T. S. (1992). *Financing Public Education in an Era of Change*. Bloomington, IN. The Phi Delta Kappa Educational Foundation.

National Association of Elementary School Principals (1990). *Principals for 21st Century Schools*. Alexandria, VA.: Author.

National Association of Secondary School Principals (1992). *Developing School Leaders: A Call for Collaboration*. Reston, VA.: Author.

National Commission for the Principalship, (1990). *Principals for Our Changing Schools*. Fairfax, VA.: Author.

Sergiovanni, T. J. (1991) *The Principalship: A Reflective Practice Perspective* (2nd ed.). Boston: Allyn and Bacon.

3

MANAGING AND CONTROLLING THE USE OF FINANCIAL RESOURCES

Managing and controlling financial resources allocated to the school imply that the school has developed a projection for the allocation and utilization of those resources. That projection typically is a plan of anticipated expenditures and is commonly referred to as the budget. The final budget representing the allocation of resources and the expected expenditures is the result of months of collaborative efforts of representatives from the staff, the community, and school leaders. Guthrie, Garms, and Pierce (1988) stated that "Budgets are the financial crystallization of an organization's intentions. It is through budgeting that decisions are made about how to allocate resources to achieve goals" (p. 216).

Managing and controlling financial resources to ensure achieving the highest return on their use require that the effective school leader be prepared in all the areas related to the development and management of the school budget. They also require that the principal take a leadership role in the education of the staff and the community in the budgeting process.

In assuming that leadership role, the principal must first

develop the school budget-planning calendar. The budget planning calendar includes timelines for the staff to follow when ordering supplies, materials, equipment, or services. When the staff follows timelines, district purchasing personnel have ample time to initiate purchase orders which, in turn, ensure timely delivery of the product to the school.

The effective school leader must be knowledgeable of the funding sources and the specific operational areas in which the funds can be utilized. The principal must educate the staff and community representatives on the aspects of school finance in such areas as school funding and school financial operations.

The school leader periodically must monitor expenditures and gather up-to-date information on encumbered funds and fund balances and must always have a plan to assist the school staff in meeting emergency situations that may arise during the school year. Such a plan requires that the school leader be fully aware of which funds can be transferred from one function or operational code to another. It requires that the school leader, whenever possible, have contingency funds available or be knowledgeable of potential sources of contingency funds. Establishing contingency fund balances, particularly at the beginning of the budget development year, requires that the principal: (1) understand the rationale for creating the contingency fund balance, and (2) be skilled in articulating that rationale to the school decision makers in the budget development process.

Finally, as has been stated previously in the first two chapters, school leaders are responsible for the wise, prudent, and effective use of financial resources allocated to the school. Inherent in this responsibility is providing skilled leadership and direction to the school planning team's assessment of the degree to which the school's goals have been achieved and the extent to which the financial resources allocated to the achievement of the school goals were effectively used. The resource allocation and reallocation process is driven by the goals that the school leader and the school planning team establish to meet the learning needs of students and the degree to which those goals are met each year. This chapter addresses these and other important budgetary considerations.

MANAGING FINANCIAL RESOURCES

THE SCHOOL BUDGET

Developing the school budget is a complex process. Caldwell and Spinks (1986) state that school-site budgeting is more complex than district-level budgeting and that principals must understand and employ line-item and work-flow budgets. The former ensures proper spending; the latter enables on-site alterations in program decisions. Budgeting is a cooperative effort involving administrators, department heads, instructional staff, service area supervisors, classified staff, the district business office, the superintendent, and the governing board. A number of factors impact on the development of the budget. Employee salaries may account for 85% to 90% of the total budget, with approximately 90% of the operational budget allocated to classroom teacher salaries. Budgeting for classroom teacher salaries is based primarily on two factors: student registration data and the projections of teacher staffing needs made by either the school or the district or both. Other factors impacting the development of the budget include specific statutory timelines for notifying employees of non-renewal of contract, the statutory timelines required of governing boards to allow for public discussion of the budget, and the statutory timelines required of boards for final approval of the district budget.

In addition to the statutory requirements affecting the development of the budget, the school's analysis of the degree to which it has achieved existing goals, current and projected needs, and enrollment trends that may reflect a need for programmatic changes are factors that impact on developing the school budget. Programmatic changes may, in turn, lead to changes in the physical plant, additional staffing, or acquiring more up-to-date equipment. For example, the staff may conclude that enrollment trends and community expectations have created a need for another computer lab. The school budget would be affected in a number of areas such as: another classroom with appropriate wiring and lighting, additional staffing, student computers, classroom furniture, computer software, instructional supplies, and in-service education for teachers. Also, revisions of the current school improvement plan that have financial implications must also be considered.

THE BUDGET CALENDAR

It is clear that an effective school leader needs to develop and implement a calendar that enables the school staff and school planning team to undertake these critical tasks in a timely, logical, and sequential manner. In so doing, the administrator will be in a sound position to determine school needs as they relate to student learning, to set school-wide goals, to project financial needs, and to develop and submit a carefully planned school budget. Although most, if not all, districts have a district-wide budget planning calendar that the schools are expected to follow, the school leader will be wise to create a budget-planning calendar to give the school staff adequate time to prepare the school budget. This ensures that the submission of the school's budget coincides with the district budget development calendar. Districts implementing the practice of site-based decision making may be reluctant to tell or advise schools when to begin the budget planning process. Rather, the district may choose to leave that decision entirely up to the school. In either case, the school principal must schedule the review and revision of the school improvement plan so that the financial needs that emerge from the revised school improvement plan can be incorporated into the budget that the school submits to the district.

Developing and implementing a school improvement plan and developing a school-wide budget are overlapping processes and, in fact, occur on a year-round basis. The school planning team may be in the process of finalizing allocations to divisions and departments for the next school year while at the same time analyzing data, identifying needs, and beginning to determine school-wide financial needs for the year after next. In other words, the budgeting process is cyclical and includes planning, budgeting, and evaluation, all of which take place within a given time period. These important responsibilities, added to the day-to-day demands and activities, underscore the importance of the school leader demonstrating skill in organization, planning, and group dynamics while leading and working with key members of the school staff and community.

During the time the principal is managing two major school-wide calendars—the school improvement calendar and the budget development calendar—the school district will also be in the process of working through the activities specified in the district-wide budget calendar. Figure 3.1 is an example of a district-wide budget development calendar. The principal must be fully aware of the district budget calendar so that the school's budget requests are submitted in accordance with the timelines specified for the development of the district budget. In this example, the principal would note that the school's budget requests are due January 22. Knowing that the term break and winter recess may occur close to the due date suggests to the principal that, for the most part, the work required of the school planning team should be completed by the end of December.

THE SCHOOL IMPROVEMENT PLAN AND BUDGET DEVELOPMENT

The budget development process logically begins when the school planning team initiates the process of analyzing school data, setting school goals, and developing the school improvement plan. Figure 3.2 is an example of a school improvement planning calendar. The first step in developing the school improvement plan is, as suggested in Chapter 2, to analyze the school data. Inasmuch as most student achievement post-test data are obtained toward the end of the school year, the analyses of these kinds of data will occur late in the school year or early summer. Other types of data, however, can be collected and analyzed during the spring. For example, student, staff, and community surveys can be administered and tabulated from January through March. Curricular and long-term programmatic needs can be projected as student registration and class enrollment data are collected and analyzed. This process can begin as soon as registration is completed. Student behavioral data such as discipline reports, suspension records, attendance, and drop-out rates can all be prepared and ready for analysis late in the school year, perhaps in the months of April and May. Consequently, the development of the school improvement plan can begin with planning team meetings beginning during the months of February or March.

FIGURE 3.1 _____ SCHOOL DISTRICT BUDGET DEVELOPMENT CALENDAR

DATE	ACTIVITY / DESCRIPTION	RESPONSIBILITY
December 1	District officials begin site visits	District assistant superintendents
December 10	District budget committee selected; invitations mailed	Superintendent / designee
January 10	First district budget committee meeting; inservice committee	Superintendent / designee
January 15	Non-salary budget projections presented to superintendent	Superintendent's designee
January 15	Projected salary schedules presented to superintendent	Superintendent's designee
January 17	Budget committee meeting; salary schedules / school finance	Superintendent / designee
January 22	School / division budget requests due to superintendent	Division heads / principals
January 29	Budget requests consolidated; preliminary documents prepared	Superintendent / designee
January 31	Preliminary budget requests submitted to superintendent	Superintendent's designee
February 1	Capital improvement requests due to superintendent	Division heads / principals
February 7	Budget committee meeting; non-capital requests evaluated	Superintendent / designee
February 21	Budget committee meeting; capital budget requests evaluated	Superintendent / designee
March 21	Budget committee finalizes budget recommendations	Superintendent / designee
April 7	Budget committee makes budget recommendations to board	Superintendent / designee
April 8	Inform principals of budget committee recommendations	Superintendent / designee
April 21	Board study session on 19 __ 19 __ budget	Superintendent / governing board
May 5	Board study session on 19 __ 19 __ budget	Superintendent / governing board
May 19	Board study session on 19 __ 19 __ budget	Superintendent / governing board
June 2	Board study session on 19 __ 19 __ budget	Superintendent / governing board
June 16	Present final budget to governing board	Superintendent / governing board
June 30	Governing board adopts budget for 19 __ 19 __ school year	Superintendent / governing board

FIGURE 3.2 CALENDAR FOR DEVELOPING/IMPLEMENTING THE SCHOOL IMPROVEMENT PLAN

MONTH	ACTION	RESPONSIBLE
FEBRUARY	1. Convene school planning team 2. Review existing school improvement plan (if one exists) 3. Identify major areas for data collection and analysis 4. Design/modify/administer student, staff, parent & community surveys 5. Compile student registration/enrollment data/patterns 6. Review information and plans with entire school staff	1. Principal 2. School planning team 3. School planning team 4. School planning team 5. Principal 6. Principal/school planning team
MARCH	1. Review student registration/enrollment data/patterns 2. Determine impact on staffing/programmatic needs 3. Adjust as needed projected staffing/programmatic requests 4. Review findings/information with entire school staff	1. School planning team 2. Department / division chairs 3. Principal/school planning team 4. Principal/school planning team
APRIL	1. Compile survey data 2. Review findings with entire school staff	1. School planning team 2. Principal/school planning team
MAY	1. Compile student non-academic behavioral/performance data 2. Identify goals and plan agenda for summer school planning retreat 3. Compile student academic performance data 4. Identify site, complete logistical requirements for planning retreat 5. Review findings and retreat plans with entire school staff	1. School planning team 2. School planning team 3. School planning team 4. Principal/school planning team 5. Principal/school planning team

Month	Tasks	Responsibility
JUNE / JULY / AUGUST	1. School planning team retreat 2. Compare current year data with stated goals and expected levels of performance 3. Identify gap areas; develop recommended goals and expected levels of performance for next school year 4. Develop strategies for presentation of recommended goals to entire school staff 5. Develop strategies for soliciting staff input for review, revision, or approval of goals	1. School planning team 2. School planning team 3. School planning team 4. School planning team 5. School planning team
SEPTEMBER	1. School planning team present goals to entire school staff 2. Solicit staff input for review, revision, and approval of goals and expected levels of performance 3. Ask each division/department to add goals, objectives, and strategies 4. Ask each division to project needed resources and potential sources 5. Conduct pre-test assessments; collect baseline data	1. Principal/school planning team 2. Principal/school planning team 3. Principal/school planning team 4. Principal/school planning team 5. School staff
OCTOBER	1. Divisional/departmental objectives, strategies, needs identified 2. Potential resources identified 3. Divisional/departmental components of school improvement plan completed and submitted to principal/school planning team 4. Divisional/departmental plans incorporated into school-wide document 5. Review preliminary school improvement document with entire school	1. Divisional/departmental staff 2. Divisional/departmental staff 3. Divisional/departmental staff 4. Principal 5. Principal/school planning team
NOVEMBER	1. Resource requests from divisions/departments consolidated 2. School planning team meets with division/department representatives; reviews objectives, strategies, and requests for additional resources 3. School improvement plan finalized; reviewed with entire school staff	1. Principal 2. Principal/school planning team 3. Principal/school planning team
DECEMBER	1. Requests from divisions/departments prioritized 2. School-wide budget developed 3. School-wide budget presented to entire school staff	1. School planning team 2. School planning team 3. Principal/school planning team
JANUARY	1. School budget requests submitted to district	1. Principal

The effective principal also provides reminders to the school staff relative to ordering supplies and equipment. This is especially important for the staff to receive needed supplies or equipment when the school year begins. The principal must obtain critical dates for submitting purchase requisitions from the district business office and provide that information to the staff. Figure 3.3 presents a purchasing calendar that would assist staff in obtaining items or services when they are most needed. This sample calendar suggests that teachers submit requisitions before they leave school for the summer in the event there is a question about an item on the requisition that only the teacher can answer. Many districts ask that requisitions for purchases of specialized kinds of items be submitted according to a specific time frame. This enables the district purchasing staff to focus on those specialized kinds of equipment during the ordering and bidding processes. A calendar such as the one shown in Figure 3.3 also gives the school staff and particularly the classroom teacher some lead time to prepare requisitions as the school year is ending, which is or can be a very busy time for the teacher.

FIGURE 3.3 CALENDAR FOR SUBMITTING
REQUISITIONS FOR PURCHASE ORDERS

TYPE OF ITEM	REQUISITION DEADLINE DATE
Audiovisual / media equipment	May 1, 19__
Textbooks	May 1, 19__
Athletic supplies and equipment	May 7, 19__
Musical equipment/instruments	May 7, 19__
Classroom furniture	May 15, 19__
Classroom instructional equipment	May 15, 19__
Instructional supplies, office supplies, custodial supplies	May 30, 19__
Support services furniture and equipment (office desks, landscaping equipment)	June 1, 19__

MONITORING THE USE OF FINANCIAL RESOURCES

PROCEDURES FOR MONITORING

Once resources have been allocated to the divisions or departments within the school, the school leader monitors the utilization of funds. The intent of monitoring is to affirm the allocation of funds, guard against ineffective allocation, and intervene by providing appropriate resources when faced with unforeseen emergencies. Principals use both formal and informal procedures: (1) to monitor expenditures and fund balances at the department level, and (2) to monitor expenditures and fund balances at the school level. Formal monitoring procedures might be defined as the principal utilizing only the fund balance and expenditure information provided by the district and only when the information is provided by the district. In this format, the principal reviews the routine periodic reports generated by the district on a regular basis. Often information contained in these printed reports from the district is not up-to-date because the district staff, for whatever reason, has not yet charged back to the school the amounts on recently-submitted requisitions. Some districts may provide principals with on-line access to fund balances for the school. In those cases, the principal may review the account balances on a regular, pre-determined schedule. Informal procedures include any system or strategy developed and implemented by the principal that would provide more accurate, up-to-date, and timely information. Synthesis and analysis of these kinds of information are particularly useful when it becomes necessary to reallocate resources during the school year. If the school leader is to manage financial resources effectively and efficiently, resources that are unused or inappropriately allocated should be reallocated to those areas that may have been underfunded or that are experiencing an unforeseen need or emergency.

A variety of processes for periodic monitoring of expenditures and fund balances can be designed and used by the principal. For example, a file might be created for each division or department's requisitions for the current school year. Periodically, the files for each department or division are pulled with the principal reviewing the requisitions to maintain a perspective on the types of items being purchased or to detect any patterns of fund management demonstrated by the department. Some departments may have a habit of spending their entire allocation early in the school year and then asking for contingency funds toward the end of the year. On the other hand, other departments may be more conservative and refrain from spending their funds until the end of the year. This often results in the annoying practice of trying to rush purchases through during very busy times of the year. This is difficult for both the principal and district business personnel. In either case, the principal needs evidence that could be used to assist the departments to manage their allocations more effectively and efficiently.

Second, the principal should develop a summary chart for each division/department similar to Figure 3.4 where key information from each requisition is entered. Most school administrators today have software or have access to software that would simplify the process of maintaining a summary sheet for each department. Such software helps the principal design a spreadsheet containing information critical to resource management. Such information might include: (1) the requisition number, (2) the date of the requisition, (3) the items ordered, (4) the funding code, and (5) the total dollar amount of the items ordered. Using Figure 3.4 as an example, by monitoring purchases by the business education department, the principal would be aware that: (1) copy paper was a supply item used in large quantities by the department, (2) the department chair appeared to appropriately manage financial resources, since requisitions were submitted in what would appear to be an attempt to accurately forecast departmental needs, and (3) there appears to be no evidence of any emergency ordering of supplies. Such an analysis of the departmental summary provides information important to fiscal allocation; the business education department may, near the end of the year, have more copy paper than needed and might be willing to provide copy paper to another department that may have depleted its funds. This summary also informs the principal of the amount of funds encumbered by the department as well as departmental fund balances. This information is extremely valuable to the principal particularly near the end of the school year when emergencies are most likely to arise. In the event of such emergencies, the principal knows what unen-

FIGURE 3.4 ALL AMERICAN SCHOOL
BUSINESS EDUCATION DEPARTMENT SUMMARY OF REQUISITIONS
19__–19__ SCHOOL YEAR

DATE OF REQUISITION	REQUISITION NUMBER	ITEMS ORDERED	BUDGET CODE	AMOUNT
May 1	A 626543	300 reams copy machine paper	5410	$ 900
May 1	A 626544	1 gross laser printer ink cartridges	5410	288
May 7	A 716832	3 Macintosh LCII student computer stations	5830	6,000
May 7	A 832444	1 gross ball point pens, red, fine point	5410	85
October 3	A 622413	3 boxes of 6 dry erase markers, assorted colors	5410	35
November 1	A 666103	1 gross manila folders, letter size, 1/3 cut	5410	236
February 1	A 783432	200 reams copy machine paper	5410	200
April 2	A 773412	1 box computer printer paper, 8-1/2 wide, perforated on sides	5410	65
May 15	A 876981	50 reams copy machine paper	5410	150

cumbered funds remain and is in a better position to pursue the reallocation of the funds to other departments needing them.

Reallocation of resources is a critical task by which the effective school leader provides resources to divisions or departments enabling them to fulfill their objectives designed to achieve the school goals. The knowledge and skills required for this element are similar to those related to the allocation of funds. The principal must be able to assimilate information quickly, make educated decisions, and implement changes related to the allocation of funds midway through the school year. Effective principals demonstrate the ability to achieve skillfully and effectively inter-departmental collaboration to meet acute needs, shift funds between departments, and seek additional funding from other sources.

BUDGET CODIFICATION

Once the district governing board has formally adopted the budget and filed the budget with the state, the district and schools generally may expend funds only in those codes that were established in the original budget. Some states have laws, financial regulations, or policies with provisions that enable schools to transfer funds from certain codes to others. It is, therefore, imperative that the principal know which general budget areas have codes that permit intercode transfers. This, again, is critical in emergency situations when the principal learns that unusual circumstances have caused the funds in a department's budget to be depleted before the end of the school year and additional funds are needed in order to sustain the department until the end of the year. The principal who is aware of all the possibilities for fund transfers is in a position to take steps to transfer the funds and resolve the crisis.

A very simple, one-page document that can be used by the principal, department heads, and the faculty as an excellent reference tool when the need arises to request fund transfers is the Budget-Transfer Chart of Accounts. For example, in Figure 3.5, the column on the left reflects all the budget codes to which funds have been allocated to the school for the current year. In the columns to the right, budget codes are listed within which or to which funds can be transferred.

FIGURE 3.5 CHART OF PERMISSIBLE CODE TRANSFERS

CODE	DESCRIPTION	CODES PERMITTING INTERCHANGEABLE TRANSFERS OF FUNDS				
5300	SALARIES	5310: ADMINISTRATIVE CLERICAL	5320: INSTRUCTIONAL AIDE	5330: INSTRUCTIONAL CLERICAL	5340: CLERICAL OVERTIME	5440: CUSTODIAL
5400	SUPPLIES	5410 INSTRUCTIONAL	5412 OFFICE	5420: CUSTODIAL		
5600	CONTRACT SERVICES	5610 CONSULTANT	5640 EQUIPMENT REPAIR			
5700	TRAVEL	5710: TRANSPORTATION	5720: MEALS	5730: LODGING	5740: REGISTRATION FEES	5750 FIELD TRIPS
5800	CAPITAL EQUIPMENT	5810: INSTRUCTIONAL AIDS / MEDIA	5820: TEXTBOOKS	5830: LANDSCAPING	5840 CLASSROOM FURNITURE	5850 INSTRUCTIONAL EQUIPMENT
5900	CONSTRUCTION / REMODELING	5810 NEW CONSTRUCTION	5820 REMODELING			

EVALUATING THE MANAGEMENT OF FINANCIAL RESOURCES

Throughout the discussion of the allocation of resources, numerous references have been made to the effective school leader and to the school planning team. These references have been made because of the changing conditions under which today's principal is working, particularly in the area of site-based decision making. This trend, a reality in many areas, underscores the importance of the principal becoming highly skilled in the management of financial resources. LaCost and Grady (1995) noted that "the importance of administrator expertise at the site level is supported by Odden's (1992) conclusion that . . . accomplishing high levels of student achievement, [as indicated in the national goals], is quintessentially a school, not a district, function" (pp. 327–328), supports the current thrust to increase principal responsibility for allocating and monitoring resources. Should future funding programs give greater emphasis to the concept of school-based funding, as is suggested by Odden (1992), schools, rather than districts, would become the primary recipient of local, state, and federal revenues" (p. 4). Effective school leaders today and in the future must become proficient in all aspects of allocating, monitoring the use of, and evaluating the return on the investment of financial resources in the school.

EVALUATION OF FINANCIAL RESOURCE UTILIZATION

The purpose of evaluating the utilization of financial resources is to determine the degree and direction of change in the condition, status, or performance in the specific goal areas identified by the school planning team. In addition, the extent to which the financial resources allocated to that goal were efficiently and effectively utilized must also be assessed. The primary method by which this is done is through the collection and analysis of objective data that parallel the types of data that were collected and analyzed at the beginning of the school improvement process. In Chapter 2, the example of a goal was cited that was to improve student performance in reading. At the beginning of the school improvement cycle, specific scores in reading from a variety of measures were collected. At the end of the school improvement cycle, the school collects and analyzes data from the same measures. The comparison of performance levels at the time the plan was implemented and the performance levels at the end of the school year is made. The specific purpose for comparing the two sets of data is to determine if the gap between the desired performance and the actual performance that existed at the beginning of the year had been reduced by the end of the year as a result of the school's implementation of the school improvement plan. Of course, inherent in this analysis is the determination of whether or not the financial resources were allocated and utilized in an effective and efficient manner.

The goal used in Chapter 2 serves as a further example, "Students will improve their performance in reading." The school further stated that documented evidence of achieving the goal would be a 10% reduction in the number of students with a documented deficiency in reading. The school planning team first will determine whether or not the school achieved this goal. Therefore, the school will assess student performance in reading, using the same assessment measures at the end of the school year that were used at the beginning of the school year to determine the degree to which the gap was reduced. Next, the school planning team must determine if the allocation of additional discretionary funding to departments or programs, to purchase supplies, services, or equipment significantly and positively impacted the achievement of this goal. In other words, "Were the purposes for which the funds were allocated achieved?" An example of a goal/resource evaluation worksheet is suggested in Figure 3.6. This figure clearly summarizes the areas in which additional discretionary funds were allocated.

The allocations were based specifically upon the requests of the divisions or departments that evolved from their school improvement plan. At some point in the process, the school planning team will extract from the school-wide school improvement plan on a departmental basis all of the additional discretionary resources allocated to achieving Goal 1. This section of Figure 3.6 is completed by the principal, the designee, or the school planning team immediately after the allocation of resources. If the school were an elementary school, the divisions or departments could be listed as shown in Figure 3.6 or they could be

FIGURE 3.6 GOAL ACHIEVEMENT/RESOURCES ALLOCATION EVALUATION WORKSHEET

School Goal 1: Students will improve their performance in reading.

Documented Evidence of Achievement: The number of students with a documented reading deficiency will be reduced by 10 %.

DIVISION DEPRTMT GRDE LVL	5410 INST SUPPLIES	5415 OFFICE SUPPLIES	5510 TEACHER SALARIES	5520 INST AIDE SALARIES	5450 CUSTOD SUPPLIES	5900 FURN & EQUIP	5540 EQUIP REPAIR	5700 TRAVEL REG FEES	5800 CONT SERVICES	5810 INST AIDS / MEDIA	5920 TEXT BOOKS	5900 CONST	TOTAL
K - 3													
4 - 6													
7 - 8													
READ SPECIAL	$ 912	$ 350											$ 1,412
ENGLISH													
SOCIAL STUDIES													
TOTAL													

ANALYSIS OF STUDENT PERFORMANCE IN READING

PRE / POST ASSESSMENT	PRE: ACTUAL PERFORMANCE	POST: ACTUAL PERFORMANCE	DESIRED PERFORMANCE	GAP	NET GAP DIFFERENCE
DISTRICT TESTS	34 % with reading deficiency	18 % with reading deficiency	0 % with reading deficiency	34 %	16 % reduction in gap
DISTRICT TESTS			0 % with reading deficiency	18 %	

CONCLUSIONS / RECOMMENDATIONS

1. There was a 16 % reduction in the number of students with reading deficiencies; this represents a 6 % increase over targeted goal.

2. Continue programs targeting improvement in reading at the current or increased level of funding.

listed by grade level. If the school were a high school or middle school, each department that had specific strategies related to achieving the goal would be listed and the amount allocated in each funding code.

The next step in the analysis is to compare the data on student performance in reading at the beginning of the cycle and data on student performance in reading at the end of the cycle. Two significant comparisons will be made as reflected in the second section of the figure. First, the school planning team will measure growth in student performance in reading. Second, the school planning team will determine if the gap between the desired level of performance in reading and the actual performance in reading has been reduced. The final question, then, is, "Did the investment of additional funds to support the strategies in the school improvement plan achieve the desired result—a reduction in the gap between the desired and actual performance of students in reading?" If so, then the school may justifiably conclude that the funds were allocated appropriately. If the gap were not reduced, the school planning team may choose to conduct a more in-depth analysis to determine those strategies that were successful and those strategies that were not successful. The team may conduct the investigation or it may ask the divisions or departments to analyze the strategies they implemented and submit their findings to the planning team.

In either event, the information relative to what was successful as well as that information relative to what was not successful will be important as the school planning team begins the process of developing the school improvement plan for the next school year. In the illustration shown in Figure 3.6, the school achieved significant results by reducing the gap by 16%. The final section in the figure represents a concise statement of the findings and recommendations. In this example, the school planning team is recommending a continued allocation of additional discretionary funds for the next school year.

Summary

This chapter emphasized the importance of the principal providing leadership to the school staff, community representatives, and the school planning team on all aspects of budget development. Factors impacting on the development of the budget such as statutory requirements and timelines, employee salaries, district and school goals, trends in student enrollment, related programmatic changes, and changing staffing needs must be thoroughly understood by the principal. The principal, in turn, must effectively and accurately communicate to the school budget planners the influence of those significant factors on the development of the school budget and the allocation of financial resources. Realizing that the budget development process is complex and may very well overlap with other school-wide planning processes, the effective principal will develop a school-level budget planning calendar that coincides with the district calendar for budget development as well as a school improvement planning calendar that will enable the staff to keep the two processes clearly in focus. Specific examples of a district-wide budget development calendar and a calendar for school improvement planning were illustrated. In addition, an example of a calendar for submitting requisitions that could be developed and utilized by the principal to assist staff to systematically order supplies, services, or equipment was proposed.

Sound management of financial resources requires that the principal monitor regularly the expenditure of funds throughout the school. Formal as well as informal procedures for monitoring school-wide budget activities were described. Procedures such as these enable the principal to collect important and useful data and to be prepared should the need arise to reallocate funds from one source or department to another in order to resolve emergency situations. The departmental Summary of Requisitions form provides the principal with the information needed to keep abreast of departmental management of school resources. Financial resource management also requires that the principal be knowledgeable of budget codes to and from which funds can be transferred in order to effectively utilize the unused funds particularly in crisis situations. The Chart of Permissible Code Transfers serves as an excellent resource management tool both for the principal and all staff members who have budgetary responsibility.

Finally, perhaps the most significant responsibility of the school leader is the annual evaluation of the utilization of the financial resources. This encompasses an analysis of the pre- and post-performance data in those areas related to the school goals. It also includes the school planning team's assessment of the degree to which the school goals have been achieved. Incorporated into both assessments is the determination of the degree to which the financial resources were effectively and appropriately utilized and their contribution to the achievement of the school goals. The Goal Achievement/Resource Allocation Worksheet provides the principal and school planning team with a clear and succinct summary of fund allocations, goal achievement, and team conclusions and recommendations. This becomes an excellent resource document for developing the school improvement plan for the following school year and the related budgetary considerations.

FOLLOW-UP ACTIVITIES

1. Develop a school-wide, year-round, budget development calendar. Include dates, critical tasks, and persons responsible. Discuss the calendar with your administrative team, grade-level or department chairs, faculty, and site council. Ask for observations and input relative to special considerations, such as avoiding scheduling school-wide events that would prevent or interfere with developing the school budget, or the need for specific information that would facilitate preparing the budget.

2. Working with your district budget director, determine all of the budget codes to which inter-code transfers are permissible. Clarify deadline dates by which fund transfers must be requested. Determine if there are any restrictions to fund transfers and, if so, what. Prepare a document similar to Figure 3.5 and in-service your faculty, staff, and site council.

3. Develop a system for monitoring budget expenditures. Try to establish departmental or divisional spending patterns or cycles. Develop a method for determining whether or not departments or divisions "stockpile" supplies and, if so, whether or not more effective and efficient utilization of those funds or items could be made.

4. Develop a work sheet for each department or division similar to Figure 3.6. At the end of the school year, ask each to provide the information required. If standardized scores cannot be used for the grade level or department, ask for other measures such as the number of students who made a grade of "C" or higher, the number of students who failed, the number of competencies mastered, or the percentage of student absenteeism. Ask each department or grade level to discuss the results in a department or grade level chair meeting or meeting with the site council. Ask each department, division, or grade level to offer suggestions on how they plan to improve performance and the implications those strategies might have on the development of the budget.

REFERENCES

Caldwell, B., & Spinks, J. (1986). *Policy Formation and Resource Allocation*. Victoria, Australia: Deakin University. (ERIC Document Reproduction Service ED 283 264).

Guthrie, J. W., Garms, W. I., & Pierce, L. C. (1988). *School Finance and Education Policy: Enhancing Educational Efficiency, Equality, and Choice*. Englewood Cliffs, NJ: Prentice-Hall.

LaCost, B. Y., & Grady, M. L. (1995). Programs that Prepare Principals for Allocating Financial Resources at the School Site: Principals and Superintendents Respond, *Educational Considerations*, 23 (1), 20.

SUGGESTED READINGS

Aamot, K., & Piotrowski, C. (1995). Accountability and Other Causes of Total Quality Management. *School Business Affairs*, October, 1995, (61) 10, pp. 36–44.

Kansas State University College of Education (1995). *Educational Considerations*. Manhattan, KS.: Author.

National LEADership Network Study Group on Restructuring Schools. (1993). *Toward Quality in Education: The Leader's Odyssey*. Austin, TX.: Prepared by B. J. Monk.

National School Public Relations Association (1981). *Good Schools: What Makes Them Work.* Arlington, VA.: Author.

Wick, J., & Gose, K. (1994). *Improving Student Performance in Your School.* Dubuque, IA.: Kendall/Hunt.

4

THE ALLOCATION OF HUMAN RESOURCES: STAFFING FOR EDUCATIONAL PURPOSES

The view that the education of children and youth must continuously be better than before has been a basic belief of the American people. Each generation of advocates or critics of education repeats the demand for better educational programs, better pre-service teacher preparation, and better in-service education of teachers already employed in schools. Whenever the topic of educational improvement is discussed, the importance of school personnel in such improvement becomes paramount. Educational leaders consistently have emphasized the importance of human resources in providing quality education.

On one occasion, a superintendent of a large metropolitan school system was being interviewed during a live TV program. The interviewer addressed the superintendent by saying, "Your school district is a large one, and you must face many school problems; tell us about your school problems." With some hesitation the superintendent replied, "We have no school problems in our school district." After a somewhat long and awkward pause the superintendent continued, "But our district has many people of all ages, races and cultural backgrounds, and we find that these people do have problems. We view the work of our school district as helping solve these 'people problems' being encountered." The belief of this superintendent that schools are people and that educational needs are people needs serves as the basic focus of this chapter.

It is our belief that school program improvement will progress as school leaders are able to motivate people, the human resources of the school enterprise. We support the viewpoint set forth several years ago by Forrest Conner (1964), formerly executive director of the American Association of School Administrators, in his statement that, "the success of the school administrator will depend more upon his skill in selecting, improving, and dealing with the human element than upon any other factor . . . . There is no more important administrative responsibility than effective personnel administration" (p. iii). Human resources administration and program development are the keys to school effectiveness. This chapter centers on the allocation of human resources and the processes for implementing, maintaining, and improving the human resources function in schools.

STAFFING THE SCHOOL FOR EDUCATIONAL PURPOSES

School practitioners tend to agree that staffing the school is the most important task they perform. This task necessitates competency in the areas of human resources planning, recruitment, selection, orientation, and assignment. Each of these processes is discussed in this chapter or in Chapter 5; they constitute the principal's primary responsibilities in human resources deployment.

HUMAN RESOURCES PLANNING

A primary purpose of the human resources function in education is to attract, develop, and maintain an effective group of personnel who will contribute positively to the attainment of school goals. This purpose infers a planned function, one that serves as a blueprint for related processes such as recruitment and selection of personnel.

Planning for human resources allocation is imperative because it can help the school principal and others to:

1) offset uncertainty in the administration of the human resources function

2) focus on the priority objectives that guide the human resources function

3) clarify human resources options and alternatives available in human resources decision making

4) systematize the priorities for allocating human resources

5) identify personnel strengths upon which an improved educational program can be built.

The intent of human resources planning is the same as any other type of organizational planning: 1) to help decide in advance what is to be done and, 2) to clarify the school's expectations of what it wants *to be* and *to do*. The aim of human resources planning is to focus the energies of the school on the right results. When the school principal and staff use effective planning procedures, they encourage responsive administration and are more able to establish meaningful goals that promote optimal allocation of human resources.

AN OPERATIONAL PROCEDURAL MODEL FOR PLANNING

The following operational procedural model sets forth specific steps and activities for administering the human resources planning process.

Step 1 - Determining Planning Goals and Initial Structural Assumptions. The human resources function must be founded on the guiding goals of the school. These goals provide the basis for the deployment of human resources. Goals relating to programs, student services, community relationships, achievement outcomes, and others provide the focus for planning school structures and relationships. The principal, school staff, and advisory groups must answer such questions as: How is the educational program to be structured? What special services should the school provide? What organizational arrangements best provide needed services? Decisions concerning pre-school programming, vocational curricula, grade level arrangements, adult programs, year-round or semester organization, and other structural assumptions must be determined.

Step 2 - Projecting Program Structures and Forecasting Human Resources Requirements. Based upon the organizational structuring and school program/service provisions determined in Step 1, forecasting the number and types of personnel needed over a period of time is completed. In order to do so, the broad structures determined in Step 1 are further refined. Is the K–6 structure, for example, to have self-contained classrooms or is a non-graded organization to be utilized? What is a satisfactory pupil/teacher ratio for various grades and/or subject-matter areas? How are special programs in special education, early childhood education, vocational education, and other programs to be delivered? Answers to these and other questions hold specific implications for the deployment of resources. For example, if the average pupil/teacher ratio (PTR) in an elementary school of 900 pupils is set at 30 students, 30 teachers would be required. If the PTR is set at 25 students, an additional 6 teachers would be necessary. Program structuring holds major implications for budget and facility allocations as well.

FORECASTING PERSONNEL NEEDS

Transition data concerning faculty changes are of paramount importance in human resources planning as is enrollment projection information. The following discussion focuses on the application of a Markovian analysis for forecasting transitions of personnel (Webb, Montello and Norton, 1994). Figure 4.1 shows the movement of 45 professional employees in several classifications in a K–6 elementary school.

The school has 45 professional employees consisting of 13 primary-level, 6 intermediate-level, 6 upper-level, 4 special education teachers, 10 teacher aides, 4 supervisors, and 2 administrators. These employee classifications and numbers of employees are listed in columns "a" and "b" in Figure 4.1. Columns "c" through "i" represent mean percentages of employee changes. Such probabilities are based on the personnel change data occurring over the past several years. Assumptions are that

FIGURE 4.1 MARKOVIAN ANALYSIS OF PERSONNEL ATTRITION

Classification	Level	Primary	Intermediate	Upper	Special Ed.	Supervisors	Adminis.	Aides	Projection
	a	b	c	d	e	f	g	h	i
Primary	13	.70	.10	.05	—	—	—	—	10
Intermediate	6	.06	.75	.08	—	—	—	—	6
Upper	6	.05	.10	.80	—	—	—	—	6
Special Education	4	—	—	—	.75	—	—	—	3
Supervisors	4	—	—	—	—	.75	—	—	3
Administrators	2	—	—	—	—	—	1.00	—	2
Aides	10	—	—	—	—	—	—	.60	6
Exit		.19	.05	.07	.25	.25	—	.40	36

Total Staff = 45

employee transition trends will continue and that unusual events that might skew the probabilities will not occur (e.g., sudden population loss or increase due to the start-up or shut-down of a large factory in the community, unusual number of employee retirements, etc.).

Column "b" shows a .70 (70%) probability that primary teachers will remain in their positions the following year, .06 (6%) of the primary teachers will move to the intermediate grades, .05 (5%) will move to the upper grades, and .19 (19%) will leave the school next year. Similarly, the intermediate-level teachers (column "c") have a probability of .10 (10%) for moving to the primary grade level, .75 (75%) for remaining at the intermediate level, .10 (10%) for moving to the upper-level grades, and .05 (5%) will leave the school.

The forecast of employee retention is shown in column "i". Projections for each staff classification are determined by summing the products of probability factors and their current employment numbers. In the case of primary-level teachers projected as available the following year, the calculation is as follows: (.70x13) and (.10x6) and (.05x6) = 10. The projection for teacher aides is calculated as follows: (.60x10) = 6; 40% or 4 aides will leave the school next year. Forecasts for other classifications, using the same procedure, would be 6 intermediate-level teachers, 6 upper-level teachers, 3 special education teachers, 3 supervisors, and 2 administrators.

The Markovian analysis technique provides a way for the school principal to gain an overall picture of projected personnel movements at the close of each year. These results provide a basis for advanced planning of human resources needs, and as a basis for studying other assumptions related to employee attrition and projected needs.

The Markovian technique, coupled with other methods for forecasting enrollment growth and/or decline, can provide needed data for the principal and others in the determination of human resources deployment including needs, staff balance, utilization of talents, compensation, and related allocation concerns.

There are several techniques available to school leaders for forecasting student enrollments. Techniques such as cohort survival and retention percentages utilize birth rates and historical retention data to forecast probable student enrollments. However, new computer technology now makes available systems such as ones produced by Ecotran Systems, Inc., (Beachwood, Ohio), ONPASS (San Jose, California), and EDULOG (Missoula, Montana) for forecasting population trends and future school enrollments. Technology has the potential for continual improvement of forecasting methods and accuracy of predictions. Thus, the planning process for the school principal and other planners can be less burdensome and more beneficial for the effective allocation of the school's human resources.

POSITION ANALYSIS AND POSITION DESCRIPTIONS

The creation of position descriptions that set forth the responsibilities and qualifications needed by personnel in their respective roles is also an important planning task. A position description provides a clear statement of facts pertaining to the duty specifications of the position, the context in which the position takes place, and the personal qualifications required by the employee. A position description evolves from a position analysis; a scientific, in-depth analysis of a position; its constituent parts; and its surrounding conditions.

CONTENTS OF A POSITION ANALYSIS

The contents of a position analysis generally include information about:

1) The position itself—its description, responsibilities, load factors, tools required, expectations, etc.

2) Position qualifications—certifications required; special abilities needed; mental, emotional, and physical requirements; experience; judgment and leadership demands; etc.

3) Effects of the work on the employee—turnover in the position, peer relationships, stress, clientele demands, agreeable/disagreeable features, illness records, etc.

4) Schedule— activities and time allotments peculiar to the position, related work/time arrangements, production time requirements, etc.

5) Conditions of work—work load factors; climate; job hazards; job characteristics and conditions such as standing, lifting, monotony; indoor/outdoor settings; production expectations; etc.

6) Staff and line relationships—supervisional responsibilities, reporting requirements, horizontal/vertical communications, unit relationships, etc.

7) Terms of employment—salary and benefits, contractual time stipulations, growth and development opportunities and requirements, continuous employment, etc.

Position analyses benefit both the school administration and those employed in the school. Specific benefits for the school administrators are that position analyses serve as a basis for:

◆ the examination of a position

◆ the improvement of position effectiveness

◆ the determination of position qualifications

◆ knowing expected position outcomes and accountabilities

◆ understanding the effects of the work on employees

◆ coordinating the various positions within the school setting

Employees benefit as well by having a position analysis in that it serves to provide:

◆ goal direction and activity focus for those in the position

◆ an indication of the effects of the position on the employee

◆ for the assurance of employee input into the responsibilities for the position and the outcomes expected

◆ the basis for bringing about a well-organized work
· environment

An example of a position description for a classroom teacher is shown in Figure 4.2. A form outline for collecting data for a teaching position's analysis is provided in Figure 4.3.

Although position descriptions for teachers are becoming more prevalent in schools than in previous years, many schools still do not describe the responsibilities of professional teachers in writing. Legal situations, and the realization of the value of such statements in the development of human resources, have served to promote the expansion of teacher position descriptions in practice. Position descriptions for teachers have several personnel benefits; they:

♦ serve as a guide for recruiting and selecting teachers who possess specific qualifications desired in a position

♦ help the teacher to gain a clear understanding of the teaching position, its expectations, and ties to the school's stated goals

♦ provide a basis for examining the expectations of the teaching role and the standards and requirements against which performance is to be assessed

♦ clarify lines of authority and expected supervisory and reporting requirements related to the position

♦ provide the stakeholders of the school community information about teaching responsibilities and expectations of professional personnel

♦ serve as a basis for handling legal issues and professional responsibilities related to the teaching position

Step 3 - Preparation of the Human Resources Inventory-Need Requirements. An assessment of current human resources provides the basis for examining the relationship of human resources needs and the human resources inventory that presently exists. Based on forecasts from Markovian transitional strategies, enrollment forecast data, prepared position descriptions, financial allocations, and assumptions concerning actions for achieving strategic planning goals, the implementation of staffing plans is exercised by relating personnel inventory to the human resources forecast.

FIGURE 4.2 CLASSROOM TEACHER'S POSITION DESCRIPTION

TITLE: Secondary School Teacher

QUALIFICATIONS: State Teacher's Certificate for Grades 10–12

SUPERVISION
RECEIVED: School Principal

SUPERVISION
GIVEN: Aide, if assigned, students

POSITION GOAL: Guide and assist students in learning subject matter and skills that will contribute to their development as mature, able and responsible citizens

RESPONSIBILITIES: Responsibilities shall include, but not be limited to the following:

- Meet and instruct assigned classes in the locations and times designated

- Plan a program of study that meets the individual needs, interests and abilities of the students in accordance with State and District requirements for curriculum

- Create a classroom environment that is conducive to learning and appropriate to the maturity and interests of the students

- Prepare for assigned classes. Show written evidence of instructional planning following established District format

- Guide the learning process toward the achievement of curriculum goals, based on these lessons, units, projects, etc.

- Encourage students to set and maintain acceptable standards of classroom behavior

- Employ a variety of instructional techniques and instructional media, consistent with the physical limitations of the location provided and the needs and capabilities of the students

- Assist students to become self-directed learners

- Understand and apply knowledge about student growth and development in order to provide maximum student learning

- Implement the District's philosophy of education, the instructional goals and objectives

- Participate in school goal setting, achievement and assessment

- Assess the accomplishments of students on a regular basis and provide progress reports as required

- Recognize the learning disabilities of students and provide an appropriate instructional program to meet those needs

- Enforce safety precautions and guidelines to protect students, equipment, materials and facilities

- Maintain accurate, complete and correct records as required by law, District policy and administrative regulations

- Assist the administration in implementing all policies and rules governing student behavior and conduct. For the classroom, develop reasonable rules of classroom behavior and procedure, and maintain order in the classroom in a fair and equitable manner

- Make provisions to be available for educational related purposes outside the instructional day when required or requested

- Plan and supervise purposeful assignments for teacher aide (s) and volunteer (s) and provide input on aide/volunteer performance

- Maintain and improve personal/professional competence

- Attend staff meetings and serve on district/ school committees as required

- Prepare substitute handbook and lesson plans in a timely manner

- Enforce and follow the policies and administrative regulations of the district

- Perform all duties as assigned

KNOWLEDGE/
SKILLS: Skills in the following teaching areas:

Instructional Skills, Planning Skills, Knowledge and Use of Materials, Knowledge of Content, Classroom Management Skills, Human Relations, Personal/Professional Skills

SPECIAL CRITERIA: Professional appearance and demeanor

TERMS OF
EMPLOYMENT: Salary: To be established by the Board on an annual basis

                       Work Year: To be established by the Board on an annual basis

                       Benefits: To be established by the Board on an annual basis

EVALUATION: Performance of this position will be evaluated in accordance with provisions of the Board's policy on Evaluation of Professional Staff (GCN)

APPROVED:

FIGURE 4.3 POSITION ANALYSIS OUTLINE FORM

POSITION DESCRIPTION ANALYSIS SHEET
Position Title:_____

Nature of Work:

Typical Duties:

Skills/Knowledge:

Educ./Training:

Experience Required:

Supervision Required:

Supervision Given:

Other:

This examination makes it possible to proceed with the task of matching position needs and qualified individuals; the recruitment and selection processes are administered.

Recruitment and selection of personnel, as related to human resources deployment, are discussed later in the chapter.

Step 4 - Evaluating the Results of the Staffing Plans. In the final phase of human resources planning, the school principal and others must evaluate the appropriateness of the plans in meeting expressed needs. Effective control procedures provide the school leaders with needed data and valuable information about successes, problems, and failures associated with the planning process, and about major disparities between the goals and objectives originally determined and the actual results.

RECRUITMENT OF HUMAN RESOURCES

Recruitment is a planned process by which personnel are informed of position openings and the potential characteristics and qualifications of applicants assessed. The process constitutes a systematic procedure for establishing a "pool" of qualified persons interested in teaching in the school. Effective recruitment practices recognize that the establishment of a pool of human resources is not merely a matter of luck; instead, there is a close relationship between planning and educational returns associated with the process. The recruitment planning process is dependent upon the outcomes of several activities in the human resources planning process previously discussed (e.g., forecasts of personnel needs, position descriptions, program organization assumptions, etc.).

The recruitment process encompasses the tasks of:

1) studying position descriptions

2) announcing position openings

3) locating sources for possible applicants, and identifying potentially qualified persons

4) implementing preliminary application procedures and collecting initial applicant information

5) initiating paper screening and completing preliminary reviews of applicants' qualifications.

Thus, the recruitment process ties closely to the human resources planning process and blends into the process of selection whereby applicants, who have survived preliminary screening and become eligible for the applicant pool, are subjected to more intensive screening procedures. Figure 4.4 illustrates the conceptual interrelationships that exist among the planning, recruitment, and selection processes.

AN OPERATIONAL MODEL FOR THE RECRUITMENT PROCESS

The following model sets forth procedures for administering an effective recruitment process. The model encompasses important steps in the planning, organizing, developing recruitment sources, recruiting activities, processing of applicants, and evaluating recruitment procedures.

Step 1 - Planning for the Recruitment of Human Resources. It is essential at the outset that the school principal leads in the development of recruitment plans. Although recruitment is a process that is often shared by the central human resources office, site-based decision making tends to place an increasing responsibility for recruitment at the local school level. In the planning stages, recruitment purposes are determined. For example, position descriptions and other personnel goals set forth in the school's strategic planning assumptions are fully discussed (e.g., staff balance, long and short-term school objectives, personnel talent losses, etc.). Policies are developed or reviewed that make possible a level of human performance consistent with the cultural make-up and function of the school. A viable school recruitment policy focuses on the aim of the process and serves to answer the question, "What is it that we want the recruitment process to accomplish?" An example of a partial recruitment policy statement is presented in Figure 4.5.

Recruitment planning necessitates attention to those activities needed to activate the plan, including the assignment of responsibilities and budgeting considerations. It is clear, for example, that recruitment on a broad basis and the use of a variety of sources, as set forth in the following policy (Figure 4.5), will require funding for advertising, necessary travel, printing of materials, secretarial services and, in some cases, released time for personnel involved in the process.

Figure 4.4 Relationship Among the Planning, Recruitment, and Selection Processes

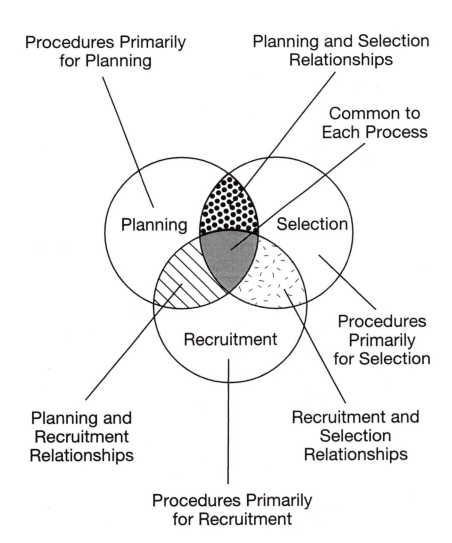

FIGURE 4.5 PERSONNEL RECRUITMENT POLICY

CODE 4112

In an effort to develop a pool of the best qualified personnel for positions at College View High School, efforts will be taken to gain a balance in staffing relative to such factors as preparation, experience, cultural background, and gender. Recruitment will be on a broad basis and available supplies of personnel for school positions will include a variety of sources such as placement bureaus, media advertisement, student teaching, staff referrals, career day activities, recruitment letters, and others that serve to identify qualified applicants and help achieve staff balance. A variety of persons will be involved in the recruitment process.

19_____ Ref: Statute 15-000

Step 2 - The Organization of Recruitment Activities. Specific responsibilities and task assignments for recruiting must be determined. This consideration includes clear definitions of the responsibilities of the local school staff and the central human resources unit. In many school districts, the recruitment and pre-screening of applicants are assumed primarily by the central personnel office of the school district. As site-based decision making expands as a school governance procedure, recruitment likely will be a responsibility assumed by the local school to a much greater extent. In any case, the organization of recruitment activities and the assignment of specific recruitment responsibilities in the process are paramount. More information concerning the establishment of an applicant pool is discussed later.

Step 3 - The Determination of Recruitment Sources - Applicant Searches. Although most schools have identified viable sources of personnel supply throughout the years, these sources frequently must be altered due to changes in supply and demand or to meet new program needs. Studies show that recruitment at university placement offices is one of the best sources for new personnel. And, although "walk-ins" often provide a sufficient number of applicants, they may not meet the need to recruit on a broad basis or provide the staff balances desired. The following listing suggests a variety of applicant supply sources available to personnel recruiters.

- ◆ university placement offices
- ◆ media, newspaper, journal advertisements
- ◆ commercial placement offices
- ◆ student teacher programs
- ◆ local talent, ex-teachers
- ◆ university faculty recommendations
- ◆ alternative certification graduates
- ◆ Future Teachers of America Chapters
- ◆ personnel directors in other school districts
- ◆ staff referrals
- ◆ recruiting letters to colleagues
- ◆ letters to schools that must RIF personnel
- ◆ transfer of current staff personnel
- ◆ teachers' association services
- ◆ use of executive search specialists

Step 4 - Establishing the Applicant Pool. A variety of activities is implemented to encourage highly qualified personnel to become applicants for school position openings. As previously noted, recruitment ties closely to the position descriptions and to the specific recruitment criteria developed in the earlier planning stages.

The accomplishment of a qualified applicant pool is the result of an effective program of recruitment. To achieve this end, the school principal and members of the recruitment team must not only locate qualified applicants, but must be prepared to process the applications received and to expedite related recruitment activities.

THE EMPLOYMENT APPLICATION—DATA GATHERING DURING THE RECRUITMENT PROCESS

Initial screening strategies, including the collection of applications, resumes, and proof of certification, are essential to establish a viable applicant pool.

The central personnel office frequently performs these pre-screening activities. Although the employment application form differs among school districts, it generally includes:

- a statement of non-discrimination
- applicant information—including name, address, teaching major/minor, special subject areas, certifications
- date of availability
- reason for leaving present position
- professional preparation history, including degrees earned, GPAs, college activities
- student teaching record
- teaching experience history
- other work experience
- special talents
- professional activities, memberships, participation
- co-curricular activities the applicant can supervise
- special honors, community and civic activities
- personal references

PROFESSIONAL PHILOSOPHY AND PERSONAL DEVELOPMENT INFORMATION

Frequently, applicants are asked to respond briefly to questions intended to assess their personal attitude and perspective. "Why do you want to teach at College View High School?," "What is your approach to student discipline?," and "How do you provide for individual student needs in your subject area or grade level?," are examples of such questions. Similar recruitment screening techniques include the use of pre-application assessment instruments. For example, prospective applicants are asked to complete a self-assessment on a series of questions in areas of high importance to the school's objectives. Following a brief summary of the school's goals, community make-up, and benefits, the prospective applicant uses the printed question-naire to complete a "self-analysis" designed to focus his/her interests and qualifications on the requirements of the position. For example, questions related to the applicant's qualifications for teaching reading in a subject-matter area, the willingness to make home visitations, individualization of instruction, or will-ingness to work as a team member might be posed. The pre-screening instrument is scored by the prospect, but results are *not* forwarded to the school in question; results are used for re-flection purposes by the applicant in order to gain a perspective concerning the expectations of the school and his/her own in-terests and qualifications. A low score on the instrument would indicate a "poor fit" between the applicant and the school posi-tion. Although an application could be completed and sent to the school, it is unlikely that the applicant would achieve suc-cess in the position if results on the self-screening instrument were negative.

Principals and other members of the recruitment team might utilize a variety of other activities to enhance the recruitment of personnel such as:

1) Developing a videotape that tells the quality of the school, the staff, and the school's programs. Have the videotape placed in appropriate teacher placement offices. Also, a school binder that highlights school programs, successes and traditions, opportunities and benefits could be made available in placement centers.

2) Installing a dial-a-job line telephone service. The line could be operative throughout the school year or on special occasions such as career days, Education Week, or during the height of recruitment activities. Use the line to announce position openings, accept verbal applications, and to state application procedures.

3) Developing a viable student teaching program for the school and working diligently to attract applicants to student teach in the school.

4) Organizing a Future Teàchers of America club in the school or school district. Encourage top students to learn about their opportunities in education as a career.

5) Using appropriate media and publications to advertise position openings. Include basic information regarding the position requirements, qualifications, compensation and benefits, application procedures and so forth.

6) Keeping a close working relationship with productive sources of applicants.

7) Keeping a good record of the graduating institutions of the school district's and school's present staff. Use this information to attract others from these same institutions.

Step 5 - Preliminary Evaluation and Processing of Applicants. The establishment of a recruitment pool of qualified applicants who are interested in joining the school staff necessitates a system of all information gathered through internal and external contacts with prospective candidates. Procedures for organizing the information gathered and a procedure for evaluating the applicants' qualifications and appropriateness for placement in the recruitment pool must be administered.

Throughout the pre-screening activities, a means for keeping applicants informed about their current status in the process, and to answer questions from them that inevitably arise, is essential. Computer technology can be utilized for developing and mailing appropriate communications. Advisements relating to the receipt of applications and the need to receive other materials (e.g., references, teaching certificates, transcripts, etc.) are expedited by the use of a microcomputer and an appropriate data base. Software packages are now available that serve to ease the burden of this necessary communication.

THE RECRUITMENT INTERVIEW

Recruitment interviews are achieved through the use of a variety of creative approaches. It is not unusual for the first recruitment contact to serve as a preliminary interview as well. The primary purpose of the recruitment interview is to help determine the "fit of the applicant" with the school and the specific position opening. Also, such interviews can serve to clarify, extend, and/or to verify information in the applicant's file to date. Preliminary observations concerning the applicant's personal characteristics can be noted for later follow-up. And, in some cases, the recruitment interview serves to corroborate certain judgments gained from the applicant's file or serves to provide information that leads to the decision not to include him/her in the applicant pool.

Figures 4.6 and 4.7 are examples of recruitment interviews based upon questions important to the school's personnel needs. Recruitment interviews typically are conducted in person, although telephone interviews are also utilized.

THE EVALUATION OF APPLICANTS—PAPER SCREENING

Considerable attention must be given to the rating of each applicant in relation to desired qualifications and to personal qualities and characteristics (e.g., enthusiasm, oral/written communication skills, professional attitudes, poise, preparation, special talents, previous success, etc.). Some procedure for examining the information gathered and reaching consensus about the applicant's qualifications and desirability for placement in the recruitment pool must be exercised. Consensus leads to a recommendation either to place or not to place the applicant in the pool. In some cases, placement priority is established; ratings of 1st, 2nd, or 3rd are given each applicant. Such ratings serve to facilitate decisions about follow-up selection activities. Those applicants who receive favorable decisions about their placement in the pool are so notified; follow-up selection procedures also are communicated at this time.

FIGURE 4.6 RECRUITING INTERVIEW

Name _____ Recruiter _____ Location_____
Date _____ Degree(s) _____ Major _____ Minor_____

1. How would you determine the students' instructional levels?

2. What two or three instructional methods do you prefer? Why?

3. What techniques would you use for classroom management?

4. What materials do you use in your teaching?

5. If you could change these materials, what would you change?

6. What do you believe are your teaching strengths?

7. How would you meet the needs of the total students? (academic, physical, social, emotional)

Comments on applicant's presentation of answers, speech patterns, use of grammar, voice, etc.

GENERAL COMMENTS

Recruiter Recommendation:

Outstanding _____ Good _____ Average_____ Poor _____

FIGURE 4.7 INTERVIEW QUESTIONS
TEACHER POOL
APRIL 19__

CANDIDATE: _____

	CONTENT RATING	PRESENTATION/ COMMUNICATION RATING
1. What Components Are Necessary For A Team To Work Well Together?	1 2 3 4 5	1 2 3 4 5
2. How Do You Plan To Involve Parents In Your Program?	1 2 3 4 5	1 2 3 4 5
3. Tell Us Your Thoughts About Classroom Management.	1 2 3 4 5	1 2 3 4 5
4. How Do You Provide For Individual Differences In Your Classroom?	1 2 3 4 5	1 2 3 4 5
5. What Monitoring Systems Would You Implement To Ensure Students Meet Year-End Expectations?	1 2 3 4 5	1 2 3 4 5
6. The District Values An Integrated Language Arts Approach; How Will You Implement This In Your Program?	1 2 3 4 5	1 2 3 4 5

Questions/Comments: _____
_____
_____
_____
_____
_____

INTERVIEWER	DATE	TOTAL POINTS CONTENT	TOTAL POINTS PRESEN/COMM.

SELECTION OF PERSONNEL

Personnel selection is a decision-making process in which one individual is chosen to fill a position on the basis of how well his/her qualifications match the requirements of the position. Teacher selection has four central purposes:

1) to determine among candidates the one of "best fit" for the position to be filled

2) to make possible a level of school operation consistent with the nature and function of the school

3) to reduce the need for retraining costs

4) to reduce the number of personnel problems with which the principal and others must contend.

Personnel selections based primarily on the subjective judgments of various individuals have proven far less than satisfactory. The literature points out instances where a candidate was rated from first to sixth choice by six different administrators. Also, pre-employment selection ratings frequently have negative correlations with the performance ratings of individuals on the job. For these reasons and others, personnel administrators have attempted to make selection of employees more objective. Examples of such efforts are presented throughout the following discussion.

The operations model that follows serves to focus the selection process on planned, organized and objective activities.

OPERATIONS MODEL FOR PERSONNEL SELECTION

Step 1 - Organizing the Selection Process—Goals, Procedures, and Assignments. Goals that guide the selection process evolve directly from selection policies adopted by the school board or by the local site-based governing council that has been delegated such authority. Figure 4.8 is an example of a partial policy for personnel selection.

Policies for selection of personnel serve the same purposes as policies in other governance areas; they are statements of decisions, principles, or aims that guide the overall procedures.

FIGURE 4.8 POLICY FOR PERSONNEL SELECTION
CODE 4001

Code 4001

The school principal and other persons delegated by the principal are authorized to determine the human resources needs of the school and, in cooperation with the central personnel unit, establish a recruitment pool from which qualified personnel will be recommended to the board for employment. The school board will employ persons best qualified for the position to be filled. Each school shall make special efforts to maintain staff balances relative to preparation, experience, gender, race and personal background.

The school principal or central personnel unit will assure that each person nominated for employment shall hold appropriate certifications for respective positions and that appropriate background checks have been ordered and evaluated.

Finalization of employment of any person becomes official when a contract is signed by that person, the background check has cleared proper evaluation, and the governing board has approved the appointment.

Selection policies provide a foundation for the school principal to develop operational procedures or regulations and are implemented through actions of school leadership and the delegation of responsibilities relating to specific selection activity assignments.

Step 2 - Establishing Selection Criteria, Selecting Appraisal Devices, and Compiling Appraisal Data. Although the position description serves a vital role in the selection process, it may differ from selection criteria utilized to rate each candidate for employment. Selection criteria set forth the desirable qualifications and characteristics needed by an individual for successful performance in a position. They include specific qualities relating to personal characteristics (e.g., appearance, sensitivity, educational values, enthusiasm, attitude, poise, etc.), professional competencies (e.g., scholarly ability, knowledge of teaching, student relationships, oral and written communication skills, judgment, etc.), and educational preparation and experience (e.g., teaching experience, certifications, professional participation, honors and awards, multicultural experiences, etc.).

Criteria for selection in some instances are weighted according to those qualifications most highly desired in a position; those qualifications considered most important for successful job performance. Several studies of the characteristics viewed as highly important by principals in teacher selection have been conducted. A recent study by Kowalski, McDaniel, Place, and Reitzug (1992) sets forth 46 characteristics that principals considered most essential in the selection of teachers. Figure 4.9 reveals the results of this study; note that only the first 21 characteristics are listed in rank order.

Owen (1984) suggested the use of a profile technique for selection purposes. Each candidate for a specific teaching position is rated numerically on a scale of 0 to 10 on those qualifications viewed most important for the position (e.g., competencies and personal characteristics). If, for example, knowledge of subject matter is considered of high importance for the position, candidates with master's degrees in the subject area, high grade-point averages in the subject, good student achievement records, and successful teaching experience in the subject area likely would receive a high rating for the knowledge criterion. Position profiles are plotted for each candidate for all of the selection criteria to find the candidate best suited for the position in question.

Evidence for selection of personnel should be gathered from a wide variety of sources. Sources available for gathering selection data include:

1) Materials—Credentials from placement offices, references, transcripts, interview reports, student teaching performance records, writing samples, and others.

2) Special Records—Grade point averages, health records, background checks, and work experience summary records.

3) Special Testing Results—National Teachers Examination, SAT, locally designed tests such as classroom management tests, content area tests, and so forth.

FIGURE 4.9 IMPORTANT CHARACTERISTICS FOR TEACHER SELECTION AS VIEWED BY PRINCIPALS

Characteristic	Mean Score (1 - low, 5 - high)
1. Respect for students	4.94
2. Honesty	4.88
3. Ability to work with peers	4.80
4. Verbal communication	4.79
5. Quality of previous experience	4.79
6. Emotional stability	4.69
7. Commitment to the teaching profession	4.69
8. Professional commitment	4.69
9. Ability to assess pupil progress	4.68
10. Professional pride	4.60
11. Willingness to be a team player	4.58
12. Effective discipline	4.54
13. Written communication	4.54
14. Ability to retain confidentiality	4.53
15. Knowledge of child growth and development	4.47
16. Understanding of subject matter	4.46
17. Ability to use questioning techniques	4.44
18. Pleasant personality	4.41
19. "Model" of several models of teaching	4.37
20. Ability to be a decision maker	4.35
21. Potential for professional growth	4.32

Source: *Factors that Principals Consider Most Important in Selecting New Teachers*, (1992). T.J. Kowalski, P. McDaniel, A.W. Place, and U.C. Reitzug. ERS Spectrum, 10(2), pp. 34–38.

4) Personal Interview Analysis—Teacher Perceiver Structured Interview, recruitment/selection interview data, and comprehensive background interview to assess personal motivation, sensitivity, range of interests, and so forth.

5) Observation Of Teaching—Actual Teaching Observations, use of videotapes of teaching performance, structural teaching situations at time of on-site visit.

6) Experience Data—Evidence of creative talents, extracurricular experiences, student relationship evidence (references, structured interviews, observed teaching, etc.), and job experiences outside of education.

Step 3 - Completion of Selection Interviews, Compilation of Selection Data, and Analyses of All Relevant Information and Data. All of the selection information and data must be organized and appropriately analyzed. The personal interview is considered one of the most important information/data sources for selection purposes. In fact, the personal interview, along with student teaching performance reports and past employer references, rates highest for gaining selection information for both experienced and inexperienced teacher candidates.

THE INTERVIEW

Interview procedures and strategies are many and varied. Previously, we discussed the nature and purposes of the recruitment interview. Its primary purpose was to determine the "fit" of the candidate with the school and position opening along with preliminary assessments of motivation, oral communication skills, and other personal characteristics.

Among the purposes of the selection interview are:

1) to assess the candidate's personal characteristics in detail

2) to learn of the candidate's educational philosophy and personal attitudes toward teaching and teaching as a career

3) to examine the candidate's understandings of instruction and learning

4) to explore information, beyond that revealed in prior application materials and activities, relative to experience and preparation

5) to gain first-hand information such as the candidate's personal skills in oral communication.

The popularity of the interview is due in large part to the fact that it is a relatively convenient procedure; it presents no special problems. The interview is not particularly time-consuming; a skilled interviewer can interview many candidates in one day. The interview can be structured to assess many important teaching skills. For example, personal motivation can be assessed through feedback received from the candidate relative to previous and future career pursuits. Other personal characteristics such as sensitivity, educational values, range of interests, stress tolerance, and oral communication can be assessed in personal interviews as well. The wide use of the selection interview also is due in part to the confidence most all interviewers place in their ability to judge people. Although evidence suggests that not all persons possess selection skills, most are confident that their ability to do so is high. The number and types of interviews utilized for selection purposes vary among schools and school districts. Selected types of selection interviews are described in the following section.

THE BEHAVIORAL INTERVIEW

The behavioral interview focuses on the specific criteria set forth in the position analysis. The selection criteria specified in the position analysis serve as the basis for assessing the candidate's "fit" concerning required competencies, personal characteristics, and appropriate experiences. Questions posed during the interview are structured specifically to gain evidence needed for the assessment. Figure 4.10 illustrates a completed behavioral interview report form based on a position analysis for a teaching position in 10th-grade English.

TALENT ATTRACTION AND SELECTION SYSTEM INTERVIEW

Following the implementation of advertising designed to gain the attention of the specially talented applicant, a brief tele-

FIGURE 4.10 BEHAVIOR INTERVIEW REPORT FORM

Candidate's Name: _____
Interviewed for Position of: _____
Interviewer(s): _____
Date: _____

1. Screening Dimension Number 1 - Knowledge of Subject Matter
    a. Degrees and Majors / Minors
    b. GPAs in English Courses
    c. Knowledge of English Curriculum
    d. Knowledge of Teaching / Learning Methodology in English
    e. Knowledge of Specific Subject(s) to be Taught (e.g., literature, communication skills, grammar, English composition).

2. Screening Dimension Number 2 - Experience and Preparation

    (**Note:** The following interview findings represent extensions and clarifications of evidence provided by other paper materials and the recruitment interview.)

    a. Specific Experiences As A Member Of A Curriculum Team in English, English Workshop, or Other In-Service Activity.
    b. Clarifications Concerning Previous Teaching Experiences in English
    c. Memberships And Participation in Professional Organizations (e.g., state and national English teachers' associations)
    d. Clarifications of Previous Teaching Experience - Areas of English Taught, Grade Levels and Methods

3. Screening Dimension Number 3 - Personal Characteristics and Qualifications
    a. Personal Appearance, Poise and Stability
    b. Communication Skills - Voice, Use of English Language, Clarity of Ideas
    c. Personality - Sensitivity
    d. Leadership Traits - Judgment, Understanding of Student Behavior, Goal Orientation.

4. Synthesis: _____
    _____
    _____

phone interview is conducted for two primary purposes: 1) to ascertain the professional qualifications of the applicant, and 2) to determine specific characteristics and qualifications of the applicant. Two or three performance-oriented questions are asked at this time (e.g., What are your perspectives on the individualization of instruction? How do you gain parental involvement concerning student support?).

Those applicants who are judged as having high potential are invited to the local school setting for follow-up performance interviews. For example, a mathematics teacher applicant might be asked to "teach us the binary system, right now." Or, an elementary school applicant for a third grade position might be asked to defend views expressed earlier concerning the self-contained classroom organization. To assess an applicant's attitudes about team building, a specific "conflict situation" might be posed for reaction (e.g., the football coach needs more time to work with the team and to travel on the days of out-of-town games. If he gets his way, you'll lose many of your students on Friday afternoons. How do you feel about that?).

Many interviewers are of the opinion that this interview technique reveals a more accurate picture of the candidate's actual behavior; he/she must react spontaneously based on current knowledge and skills.

VIDEOTAPED INTERVIEWS

A 5–10 minute video taped interview is utilized to gain knowledge about the candidate's personal attitudes and to assess oral communication skills. Since the videotape can be viewed by others on the selection team who are more detached personally, more objectivity is possible. Too, the interview can be viewed as many times as necessary.

THE GROUP INTERVIEW

More emphasis is being given to interviews in group settings. A typical procedure is the selection of a representative committee that completes necessary paper screening of applicants and then recommends the finalists to be interviewed. Finalist candidates spend perhaps a day interacting with teachers, students, committee members, and others. Typically, consensus assessments determine candidate ratings and the committee recommendations sent to the principal.

The group interview process allows for broader involvement of individuals in the selection process, permits the observation of the candidate in a variety of settings, and provides opportunities for a broad spectrum of questions to be addressed.

THE STRUCTURED INTERVIEW

The structured interview represents a specific effort to gain more objectivity in the selection process and to gain knowledge about the candidate relative to specific qualities desired in the position. The structured interview consists of a set of prepared questions that are asked of each candidate. Most often, the structured interview has pre-determined "look-fors" as desired responses. For example, if rapport with students is a primary characteristic desired for a position, several questions would focus on this behavior. Similarly, three or four questions might focus on empathy, others on desired traits such as mission, educational values, flexibility, and so forth.

Look-fors in structured interviews may evolve from characteristics in the position analysis, established selection criteria as discussed previously, or through research that has focused on "master teachers" who tend to respond to the same questions in a specific, consistent way. Since structured interviews most often are conducted one-on-one, interviewers typically are trained and certified in the procedure, thus inter-rater reliability is enhanced considerably.

THE INTERVIEW REPORT FORM

The format of the interview report form varies according to the type of interview. In any case, some summary report of interview results is essential. Figure 4.11 presents an example of a general report form. Although the interviewer will likely have more extensive notes from the interview, the interview report form serves to summarize primary information, results, and evaluation ratings. It is made available to all other members of the selection team.

FIGURE 4.11 INTERVIEW SUMMARY REPORT

Date _____

Desired Position: _____

El. _____ Jr. _____ Sr. _____ or Other _____

Interviewed at: College _____

Personnel Office _____

Credentials: Complete _____ Incomplete _____

Interviewer Signature _____

I. Personal Data

    Mr.
    Miss
Name   Mrs. _____   _____   _____
              Last   First   Middle

Address _____ _____ _____   Phone _____
                City   State   Zip

II. College Data

BA ____ MA ____ DR ____ College _____ Date _____ Certification _____

Where student taught _____ Subject _____ Grade _____ Year _____

Teaching Endorsements: _____ hrs _____ , _____ hrs _____ . G.P.A. _____

III. Teaching or Related Experience (Give type and length) _____

IV. Traits:

Key: 1 - Exceptional, 2 - Excellent, 3 - Good, 4 - Fair, 5 - Poor.

	1 2 3 4 5	Comments
Appearance - Grooming, Neatness, Appropriate Dress		
Personality - Poise - Enthusiasm		
English - Speech - Articulation		
Quality of Questions and Answers		
Emotional Stability - Maturity		
Professional Attitude		
Professional Awareness		

V. Comments: (Can you tell if applicant is creative, interested in change, a catalyst, innovative, goal oriented?) _____
_____
_____
_____

VI. Evaluation: Interview Rating: Low High 1 2 3 4 5   Credentials/References Rating: Low High 1 2 3 4 5

Personnel Office Use Only -

VII. Contract Recommendation:
Priority One _____ Priority Two _____ Priority Three _____ Not Recommended _____

VIII. Suggested Assignment: El _____ Jr _____ Sr _____ Other _____ Subject Area: _____

Regardless of the types of interviews conducted, such information, coupled with all other information gathered as to the candidate's qualifications, serves as the basis upon which objective selection judgments are founded.

Step 4 - Nominations of Finalists. Through consensus procedures determined in the early stages of planning, nominated candidates are recommended to the school principal and, in turn, to the school superintendent and school board for consideration. In most governance structures existing at present, only the school board can approve contractual agreements with prospective teachers.

At approximately this time in the selection process, a number of actions is initiated to confirm nomination recommendations for appropriate parties, to verify certification data, to verify teaching experience, to initiate payroll actions, to perform background checks, and to send letters of nomination and/or non-acceptance. Principals should coordinate these activities with their district office.

SUMMARY

The effective allocation of human resources depends upon several factors, foremost of which are the effective recruitment and selection of quality personnel for positions that have been closely analyzed concerning tasks required and qualifications needed by persons in the positions. Recruitment and selection of human resources for schools are processes requiring high-level administrative skills in planning, organizing, implementing, and evaluating procedural actions required by each.

A viable program of human resources deployment also requires attention to the utilization of personnel. Orientation practices, staff assignments, organizational climate, teacher work load and conditions of work, and staff motivation are among the practices that influence effective personnel utilization and sound human resources deployment. Chapter 5 centers on these and other human resources deployment considerations.

FOLLOW-UP ACTIVITIES

1. Gather data for your school situation concerning staff attrition over the last five `years. Consider the various staff changes as suggested in the Markovian analysis of personnel attrition presented in the chapter. Are there identifiable patterns, attrition percentages, exit data, and so forth that might enhance personnel planning for next year and the years ahead?

2. Review your present position description. Does it describe duties and responsibilities or does it center mainly on outcomes and results expected in the role? If it emphasizes position responsibilities, revise it to specify outcomes and then determine which version of the description serves better in your case.

3. For your next personnel hire, implement the procedures suggested by Owen in the chapter. That is, use the profile technique for selection purposes by determining the priority criteria relative to positive qualifications, and use the results to develop interview instruments and assessment procedures for position applicants.

4. Review the suggested operations model in the chapter concerning personnel selection. Assess your current procedures relative to the recommended ones set forth in the model. What improvements might be suggested in your current procedures?

5. In your present selection process, what strategies are in place for assessing such applicant characteristics as sensitivity, judgment, student rapport, and so forth? Re-examine chapter content relative to assessment strategies that can facilitate the assessment of such qualities.

REFERENCES

Kowalski, T. J., McDaniel, P., Place, A.W., & Reitzug, U.C. (1992). Factors that Principals Consider Most Important in Selecting New Teachers. *ERS Spectrum*, 10(2), 34–38.

Owen, P.E. (1984). Profile Analysis: Matching Positions and Personnel. *Supervisory Management*, 29(11), 14–20.

Van Zwoll, J. A. (1964). *School Personnel Administration*. New York: Appleton-Century Crofts.

SUGGESTED READINGS

Castetter, W. B. (1996). *The Human Resource Function in Educational Administration*. Englewood Cliffs, New Jersey: Prentice-Hall, Inc.

Feuer, M. J., Niehaus, R. J., & Sheridan, J. A. (1984). Human Resource Forecasting: A Survey of Practice and Potential. *Human Resource Planning*, 7(2), 85–97.

Hughes, L. W., & Ubben, G. C. (1989). *The Elementary Principal's Handbook*, (3rd ed.). Boston: Allyn and Bacon.

Milkovich, G. T., & Boudreau, J. W. (1991). *Human Resource Management*. Boston: Irwin.

Rebore, R. W. (1991). *Personnel Administration in Education: A Management Approach* (3rd ed.). Englewood Cliffs, New Jersey: Prentice-Hall.

Webb, L. D., Montello, P. A., & Norton, M. S. (1994). *Human Resources Administration: Personnel Issues and Needs in Education*, (2nd ed.). New York: Merrill, an imprint of Macmillan College Publishing Company.

5

THE ALLOCATION OF HUMAN RESOURCES: EFFECTIVE STAFF UTILIZATION

Human resources allocation has assumed a more comprehensive meaning than the traditional concept of "best fit" only. Allocation has broadened to encompass several human resources considerations:

1) deployment of human talent in the best interests of students, programs, and professional personnel

2) the identification of human talent and the assignment of employees so as to capitalize on these strengths

3) the assessment of school roles, including the identification of facilitators and inhibitors that affect optimal performance

4) the use of available research, tools and programs in order to establish a healthy climate and maximize human potential

5) provisions for human fulfillment including opportunities for meaningful work and personal development.

Chapter 5 discusses the foregoing human resources practices and emphasizes the leadership role of the school principal in the achievement of positive results.

Specifically, the overall theme of effective resource allocation is examined through discussions of staff orientation practices, personnel assignments, staffing patterns, school climate, work load and conditions of work, and staff development. The importance of the administrative responsibility for effective personnel practices is a continued theme emphasized throughout the chapter.

THE STAFF ORIENTATION PROCESS

The staff orientation process has a primary purpose of introducing new staff personnel to their responsibilities in the school and the community. Orientation serves as the linking pin between systematic recruitment and selection practices and between position assignment and subsequent professional development efforts.

The significance of effective orientation practices, as related to the allocation of human resources, has been underlined by various research studies. An early study by Berglas (1973), for example, found that orientation practices relating to personal assistance was the best single factor of all morale factors for new faculty personnel. In view of what is known about the loss of teacher talent from the profession in the early years of practice, it is evident that staff orientation practices are paramount. Some studies have found that as many as 25% of first-year teachers leave the profession after only one year, and that only 50% remain as active members of the teaching profession after five years of service. Other evidence points to the fact that only one in four teachers entering the profession will continue beyond his/her 15th year.

STAFF ORIENTATION DEFINED

Staff orientation is those activities planned and programmed to gain congruency between the goals of the school and the needs of the employee. Barnard (1938) referred to this relationship as the organization's capacity of equilibrium. Orientation begins with the first contact a potential applicant has with the school and continues as long as both the teacher and school administration deem it necessary.

PURPOSES OF STAFF ORIENTATION

Identifying the primary purposes of the staff orientation process serves to explain its importance for effective personnel allocation as well. Major purposes of orientation are to:

1) Encourage quality applicants to apply in the district. This purpose focuses on the broadened concept of orientation; it encompasses pre-employment as well as post-employment activities.

2) Assure an effective transition of new school personnel into the school and the school community, helping each employee gain the best possible start in the school position for which he/she is employed.

3) Promote the understanding of and commitment to the purposes and objectives of the school. Such commitment facilitates the achievement of school purposes and the effective allocation of human resources.

4) Reduce and/or resolve problems that inhibit employee effectiveness; efforts are made to eliminate job inhibitors.

5) Ascertain the specific needs of personnel new to the school. Such actions lead to higher staff morale and fulfillment of human potential.

6) Provide information that serves to identify human and material resources for instructional purposes. This serves to enhance the creative talents of new personnel.

7) Acquaint new employees with the school community, including the existing cultures, student demographics, and school history. New personnel must understand the school/community of which they are a part.

8) Promote high levels of personal job satisfaction and promote professional career success. Such efforts serve toward meeting personal employee needs as well as to serve organizational purposes.

Each of the foregoing purposes suggests the need for program implementation and administrative leadership. These considerations are discussed throughout the remainder of the chapter.

GUIDING PRINCIPLES FOR ORIENTATION PRACTICES

Effective staff orientation practices are supported by the following guiding principles:

1) The orientation process is a planned, comprehensive complex of activities that are based on the stated goals of the school.

2) Policies that guide and support the orientation process are adopted through responsive action of the school board and the administrative leadership of the school.

3) Primary responsibility for the coordination and implementation of the orientation process is vested in the leadership of the school's administration, although it is a shared responsibility that necessitates the cooperation of the district's personnel unit, the local professional staff, and local community representatives.

4) Programs of orientation include both individual and group activities. Orientation serves to enhance the objectives of the school and school district, and to meet the interests and needs of the employees.

Thus orientation program activities must be designed to meet the foregoing guiding principles. The following operations model sets forth procedures for implementing the process.

ORIENTATION PROCESS OPERATIONAL MODEL

The orientation process is based on four comprehensive steps that guide the implementation and establishment of an effective program.

Step 1 - The Establishment of Personnel Orientation Policies and Regulations. It is essential that the school board and/ or the local school unit adopt policies that commit the district and local schools to an effective orientation process and what it is that orientation is to accomplish.

The school district's policy statement for orientation need not be extensive. A statement to the effect that, "The College View School District's administration will provide appropriate orientation programs for all new employees," is sufficient. Orientation regulations are more detailed. Figure 5.1 illustrates an orientation regulation that sets forth the primary focus of the process, specifies information to be provided, and establishes the responsibility for its implementation.

Without directional and supportive regulations, such as the example in Figure 5.1, orientation provisions are likely to be sporadic and lacking the necessary focus.

Step 2 - Identification of Orientation Program Needs - Determination of Orientation Program Plans and Responsibilities. Effective orientation programs are those that serve both the school's objectives and the needs of individual employees. Both school objectives and employee needs necessitate orientation activities that center on the context in which a position takes place, the position responsibilities, relationships that influence the position, and the specific knowledge and competencies important for successful performance in the position. In order to provide activities that help employees to understand the context of their positions, principals must plan programs that provide specific information about the school/community setting (e.g., the community make-up; district and school policies and regulations; information about available resources, school facilities, and resource personnel; the student population; testing and grading procedures; etc.). Similarly, needs related to role respon-

FIGURE 5.1 ORIENTATION REGULATION

**Regulation
4230.1**

HUMAN RESOURCES

Orientation—Certificated Employees

System-Wide Basis

Orientation of new certificated employees will be the responsibility of the Human Resources Division with assistance by subject area consultants, district administrators and other designated staff.

School Building Basis

The principal is responsible for the orientation of new certificated employees. Principals should give information and general directions in regard to the following:

1. The names of certificated employees, the office staff, cafeteria personnel, custodians and other special staff personnel assigned to the building.
2. Physical facilities of the building.
3. Teaching materials: courses of study, guide books, textbooks, and supplementary materials for grade or subject.
4. Method of ordering books and supplies, securing audiovisual equipment, methods of getting material duplicated, disposing of lost and found articles.
5. Regulations for students in building and on school grounds; uses of entrances, exits, lavatories, playground areas, equipment and activities; regulations for students during, before, and after school hours.
6. Directions about building meetings, in-service training meetings, other meetings, assignments to school committees, fire drill regulations, policies concerning certificated employees' absence, attendance, dismissal, excuse of students from school, and procedure for suspected child abuse, etc.
7. The goals of the Lincoln Public Schools.
8. School system policies and regulations.

Date Regulation Reviewed by the Board of Education: 5-12-19__
Related Policies and Regulations:
Legal Reference:
Source: Reprinted by permission of the Lincoln, Nebraska, Public Schools.

sibilities and relationships must include information about the position itself, channels of communication, relationships between the position and other departments and individuals, and various resources and services available to the employee. Activities related to specific role competencies and required knowledge should include attention to program and subject-area curricula and objectives, student testing and evaluation, instructional support services, and conditions of work, including considerations of work load.

PROBLEMS OF BEGINNING TEACHERS

Orientation programming must give special attention to the specific problems faced by beginning teachers. Numerous studies have identified those problems/concerns common to most all new teacher personnel. Among such problems are the following:

- ◆ problems and frustration with the variety of administrative routines and accompanying paper work encountered
- ◆ concerns about the evaluation of student performance and school grading practices
- ◆ problems relating to student behavior and handling of student discipline
- ◆ problems related to teacher load and expectations for assuming extra-curricular assignments
- ◆ concerns about relationships with peers and administrative personnel, including supervisory relationships and communication channels
- ◆ concerns about the nature of the student population and becoming knowledgeable about the school community
- ◆ problems of finance; meeting the requirements of increased personal and professional expenditures on a first-year teacher's income

Once the specific orientation program needs are identified, the school principal must assume the leadership for program planning and the assignment of program responsibilities. Although all of the possible program provisions cannot be discussed here, the following step in the operational model suggests several ways in which program implementation might take place.

Step 3 - Implementation of Orientation Plans. Both group and individual programs of personnel orientation are administered in Step 3. Those persons who have been assigned responsibilities for program activities take necessary actions to implement them. As previously noted, orientation strategies are many and varied; needs, resources, past experiences, and time generally dictate the specific strategies to be utilized.

Common orientation practices are represented by the following provisions:

1. *Mentoring Arrangements* - The assignment of a mentor to a new teacher is one of the more common orientation practices. A more experienced, competent teacher serves as a resource person for the new employee. This arrangement provides a means for helping the new teacher gain information and skills concerning many of the problems of new teachers previously discussed. Effective mentors most often have received training in mentoring; they understand the role of a mentor and the methods for helping the mentee "to best help himself/herself."

2. *Policy/Regulation Manual & Personnel Information Handbook* - A viable school district policy manual can provide information about the goals, expectations, and procedures concerning district and school governance. Such information can serve the teacher's decision-making activities and also provide some confidence that personal actions are supportive of school aims. Informational handbooks provide the new teacher with readily accessible information about administrative routines, personnel rules and regulations, student discipline regulations, commu-

nication channels, professional growth requirements, available support resources, and other topics that have been identified as primary problems for new personnel.

3. *Group and Individual "Instructional Briefings"* - Special sessions that center on identified orientation needs should be scheduled periodically during the year to answer questions and suggest procedures for handling matters such as student discipline, reporting, administrative routines, policy, and others. Personal problems of new employees might best be resolved through the services of an employee assistance program (EAP). School leaders must recognize that unresolved personal problems may adversely affect the effective performance of both new and experienced personnel. To facilitate the resolution of personal problems through EAP services, new personnel must be informed of the services provided, the confidentiality of participation, and be encouraged to take advantage of EAP services.

Group and individual orientation briefings must be carefully planned and effectively presented. Although such sessions often are concentrated at the outset of a school year, they should be planned and scheduled as needed throughout the school term.

Step 4 - The Evaluation of the Orientation Program Results. Follow-up surveys, exit personnel interviews, complaint and inquiry data, and performance observations are among the information that is beneficial in evaluating the effectiveness of the orientation program. There is an adage that says, "If you want to know what people think and want to learn about their needs, just ask them." Evaluation procedures necessitate objective gathering of data concerning program outcomes, methods for analyzing the data gathered, and the utilization of findings for improving the program in the future.

An orientation program—when properly planned, organized, and implemented—helps facilitate employee productivity and personal satisfaction; it is fundamental to the effective allocation of human resources.

The Assignment of Personnel

Authorities have consistently noted that proper placement of people, where there is a productive job match and a focus on the use of personal strengths, is perhaps the most important management skill in the allocation of human resources (Coil, 1984; Drucker, 1974). Assigning teachers to positions of personal interest and qualifications seems so logical that problems relating to inappropriate assignments often go unheeded. Indeed, if appropriate screening procedures, as previously discussed in Chapter 4, have been followed, seemingly the question of appropriate staff assignment should be resolved. Yet, many factors come into play in assigning personnel that serve to reduce personnel effectiveness and militate against school goal accomplishment. Among these factors are inequities in work load assignments, a "misfit" between the employee and the leadership style of the supervisor, the inability of the teacher to adjust to the school/community culture, specific pre-service training of the teacher that differs from the local school's instructional methods, an organizational climate of the school that inhibits the implementation of creative talents, personal problems that occur on the part of the employee not anticipated at the time of hire, and so forth.

Responsibilities of the School Principal

School principals must assume several key responsibilities relative to personnel assignments.

Leadership in the development of an assignment policy that provides direction for the procedure. Although the adoption of all policies is the exclusive role of the school board, school policy development most often is carried out by the professional staff. As is the case with all policies, an assignment policy sets forth the aim of the assignment of staff, provides for the accountability of the procedure, and specifies what is to be done and/or accomplished. An example of an assignment policy is illustrated in Figure 5.2.

Figure 5.3 is an example of an assignment questionnaire that might be utilized to ascertain employees' in-grade or subject-

FIGURE 5.2 THE ASSIGNMENT OF PERSONNEL

Code 4113

The assignment of teaching personnel within a school is the responsibility of the school principal. Assignments are determined on the basis of such factors as match between the position description and employee qualifications, work load conditions, and other factors such as program needs, staff balance and student relationships. Although school seniority is a consideration in the assignment of staff personnel, it is not to be the dominant factor for assignment preferences.

Every effort will be made in the assignment of teachers to recognize personal talents and individual interests. Recognition of individual differences among professional staff members, equitable work load assignments, and student make-up should be considered in placement decisions.

In cases of proposed changes in grade or subject-area assignments for newly hired and/or continuing personnel, those affected will be consulted by the school principal.

---

area assignment changes. Requests and notifications of developing new interest areas also can be gathered through the use of such a questionnaire.

Deployment of staff talent in the best interests of the individual, students and total school staff. The benefits of assigning personnel to positions where their talents can be fully exercised have been noted previously. Effective allocation of personnel necessitates attention to:

1) the professional preparation, special talents, and personal interests of the teacher

2) the specific position assignment and the employee qualifications required for successful performance

3) the nature of the students who are to be instructed
   · and/or supervised

FIGURE 5.3 ASSIGNMENT QUESTIONNAIRE AND INTEREST ASSESSMENT

Name of Teacher: _____

Present Position: _____   _____
                     Location   Grade Level(s)

_____
                        Subjects Taught

Time at Present Location: _____

Teaching Assignment Change Being Requested:

    Grade Level Change (please explain): _____

    _____

    _____

    Subject-Area Change (please explain): _____

    _____

    _____

    Supervisory or Extra-Curricular Responsibility Change Request:

    _____

Comments/Clarifications:_____

_____

Principal's Recommendations: _____

_____

_____   _____
            Signature   Date

4) the relationships of the position assignment with other role assignments; the total program of the school and balance of faculty strengths must be considered

5) other factors such as the long-range needs of the school, career interests of school personnel, certification requirements, past teacher experiences, and school cultural considerations.

Successful allocation of human resources encompasses several administrative practices, but effective teacher assignments that focus on what is best for students and the personal strengths and interests of staff personnel serve as the foundation of positive human resources allocation.

The assignment of personnel to facilitate school staffing patterns and instructional programming. School principals hold the primary responsibility for the deployment of teachers and other personnel in order to facilitate the accomplishment of instructional objectives and program services of the school.

Staffing patterns not only "dictate" the number of personnel assigned, but hold important deployment implications for team balance, talent resources, support personnel, and student distribution. Hughes and Ubben (1989) illustrate the deployment of staff as related to team organization in a multiage grouping structure (Figure 5.4). As noted by the authors, the staffing pattern allows for an even student distribution and helps to ensure uniformity in the availability of human and instructional resources.

Program scheduling related to semester plans, year-round school programs, and other scheduling arrangements necessitate considerations for resource allocation as well.

Year-round school arrangements have returned to popularity in some areas of the nation, even though such scheduling plans have been utilized historically in education. Knezevich (1975) summarized several of the most popular year-round school organizational plans. Figure 5.5 presents a summary of several year-round plans.

FIGURE 5.4 A MULTIUNIT DESIGN FOR STAFF AND STUDENTS

Unit 4	Unit 5	Specialist Unit
4 teachers	4 teachers	1 music teacher
1 instructional aide	1 special ed. teacher	1 art teacher
½ clerical aide	1 instructional aide	2 P.E. teachers
-------------------------	½ clerical aide	1 librarian
120 children 3,4,5	----------------------------	½ clerical aide
	120 students 4,5,6	
Unit 1	Unit 2	Unit 3
4 teachers	4 teachers	4 teachers
1 instructional aide	1 instructional aide	1 special ed. teacher
½ clerical aide	½ clerical aide	1 instructional aide
-------------------------	-------------------------	½ clerical aide
120 children K, 1, 2	120 children K,1,2	----------------------------
		120 children 2,3,4

Source: L.W. Hughes & G. C. Ubben, *The Elementary Principal's Handbook*, (1989), (3rd ed.) Boston: Allyn & Bacon. Used by permission.

Differentiated staffing is practiced to some extent in most all modern schools today. Such staffing arrangements strive to deploy staff numbers and talents most efficiently and effectively in relation to student learning groups, learning styles, and special program services. Differentiated staffing patterns vary widely among schools. Figure 5.6 is one example of differentiated staffing that has emphasized special resource services, teacher talent, and variable student grouping.

Developing a positive working climate that fosters the maximization of human potential. Organizational climate is defined as the collective personality of the school; the atmosphere as characterized by the social and professional interactions of the individuals in the school. We often speak of an individual's personality. The "personality" of a school has been termed the school's syntality. School climate is interpersonal; it is reflected in the relationships, attitudes, and actions of the professional staff in the school setting.

FIGURE 5.5 YEAR-ROUND ORGANIZATIONAL ARRANGEMENTS

The Four-Quarter Plan	Four quarters with rotating attendance. Pupil vacations are staggered. Schools operate all year. Each pupil attends 9 months of school. Teachers are employed for 3 or 4 quarters.
The Trimester Plan	Three periods that encompass one-third of the school year. Schools operate all year. Each pupil attends 2 or 3 trimesters. Teachers typically teach all 3 trimesters and therefore have 12 month employment.
The 45–15 Plan	Approximately one-fourth of the students are enrolled at any one time. Vacation time is for 15 school days (3 weeks) rather than for a full quarter. Pupils attend 45 days and then have vacation for 15 days. Pattern of 45–15 is repeated four times during the year. Teachers typically are employed year-round and vacation parallels that of students (45–15).
Summer School Plan	The school operates most often for a 9 month period and typically for 2 summer terms of 6 or 7 weeks each. All students attend the 9 month regular school session. Some attend special summer sessions, depending on interests and needs. Teachers are employed for 9 months. Some volunteer for teaching during one or more summer sessions.

Source: Based on information in Administration of Public Education (1973) by S. J. Knezevich. New York: Harper & Row, Publishers.

Organizational climate is significant in a discussion of human resources allocation for several reasons:

1) The climate of the school sets the tone for the human considerations important for meeting school objectives and resolving related problems.

2) Effective school communication necessitates a climate of trust, mutual respect, and clarity of function. Communication serves to tie school personnel together; without communication, human energies are not properly focused.

3) A positive climate sets the opportunity for personal growth. Personal growth is essential for schools to remain alive and vital.

4) The climate conditions the setting for creative human effort, the generation of innovation and program change (Christian, 1972).

5) Team building in schools infers the need for a healthy school climate. Team effort requires the support of an open school climate exemplified by an environment that serves to stimulate cooperative staff efforts.

The school principal has an important role in determining what the school *is* and what it might *become*. In order to have a positive influence, however, the principal needs to consider factors that have not been given due attention previously. This consideration necessitates the examination of conditions from the viewpoints of several stakeholders—teachers, students, community members, and others. The principal must gain an understanding of why school climate is important, how school climate can be determined, and know of strategies to foster a positive environment within the school.

ASSESSMENT OF SCHOOL CLIMATE

Since research evidence supports the influence of the school principal on the school's environment, the various attempts to measure climate have tended to focus on principal/teacher relationships.

FIGURE 5.6 DIFFERENTIATED STAFFING MODEL

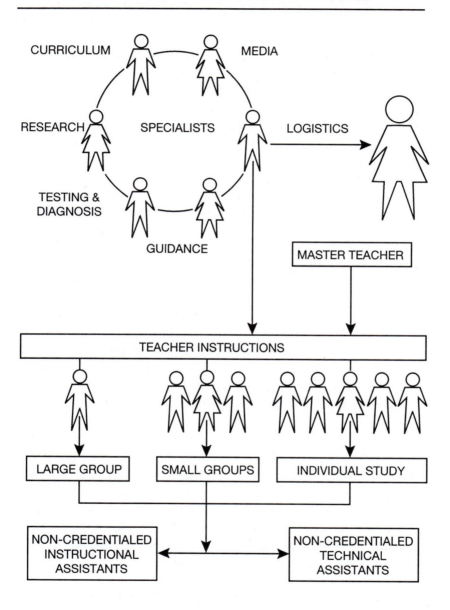

Halpin and Croft's Organizational Description Questionnaire (OCDQ, 1963) was one of the first comprehensive instruments designed to assess school climate. A profile from the subtest scores was constructed that revealed six profile-types arranged on a general continuum from open to closed. The OCDQ has been a popular means for assessing school climate. Since its development in 1963, several hundred empirical studies have utilized the OCDQ. Also, other versions of the OCDQ, such as the Organizational Climate Description Questionnaire - Revised Elementary (OCDQ-RE) (Hoy and Clover, 1986), have been developed in more recent years.

The Purdue Teacher Opinionaire (PTO, 1970) is another standardized instrument used to assess school climate. Norms have been developed for 10 areas of school environment such as teacher rapport with the principal, rapport among teachers, satisfaction with teaching, teacher status, and others. The PTO can be used by the principal to assess school morale and to examine other factors in the school closely associated with school climate.

The High School Characteristics Index (HSCI, 1964) is another example of a standardized instrument for assessing school climate. The HSCI differs from the previously mentioned instruments in that it provides a climate profile from the perspectives of the student population. Thirty scales are provided on the HSCI that relate to seven factors of school climate, including group life, personal dignity, achievement standards, orderliness, and others.

In some cases, the school principal will find it convenient to design his/her own climate assessment instrument. Although such instruments lack state or national comparative norms, these locally developed instruments can serve to gain specific information relative to perceptions of existing climate conditions. Figure 5.7 is an example of a partially localized instrument. Such instruments most often utilize simple "yes" or "no" responses or a Likert-type scale as shown in Figure 5.7.

HOW SCHOOL CLIMATE CAN BE IMPROVED

Many excellent books and journal articles have been published that focus on the importance, the measurement, and the improvement of school climate. The reader is referred to the se-

FIGURE 5.7 SCHOOLING IMPROVEMENT PRACTICE STUDY
STUDENT SCHOOL CLIMATE SURVEY

School _____
Grade _____

DIRECTIONS :

As you read each statement, please circle the number which best describes how you feel about your school. Do not circle more than one number for each statement.

Value of the number :   1) Strongly Disagree   2) Disagree
                          3) Neutral   4) Agree   5) Strongly Agree

---

I. SCHOOL ATMOSPHERE/MORALE

	Strongly Disagree	Disagree	Neutral	Agree	Strongly Agree
1. Our school has a friendly atmosphere.	1	2	3	4	5
2. Our school is a place where students want to be and a place where they can learn in a pleasant environment.	1	2	3	4	5
3. The students and staff take pride in our school.	1	2	3	4	5
4. School spirit and morale are high in our school.	1	2	3	4	5
5. Students and staff members in our school are usually happy.	1	2	3	4	5

II. STUDENT/STAFF RELATIONSHIPS

1. Staff members and students trust and respect one another.	1	2	3	4	5
2. Teachers in our school care about students and go out of their way to help them.	1	2	3	4	5

	Strongly Disagree	Disagree	Neutral	Agree	Strongly Agree
3. Teachers and other school personel in our school treat students fairly and as persons.	1	2	3	4	5
4. Students and staff in our school frequently participate in activities that solve problems and improve our school,	1	2	3	4	5
5. The principal of our school is respected by students and staff members and is looked upon as an effective leader.	1	2	3	4	5

III. STUDENT BEHAVIOR/SCHOOL RULES

1. There are relatively few discipline problems in our school.	1	2	3	4	5
2. The rules in our school are clearly defined and fair.	1	2	3	4	5
3. Most students in our school obey the school rules.	1	2	3	4	5
4. The attendance is good in our school.	1	2	3	4	5
5. Visitors in our school consider our students well-behaved and courteous.	1	2	3	4	5

IV. PEER RELATIONSHIPS

1. The students in our school get along well with each other.	1	2	3	4	5
2. All students in our school are treated with respect regardless of race, religion, physical, or mental handicaps.	1	2	3	4	5
3. Students in our schools are willing to give a helping hand to other students.	1	2	3	4	5
4. There is little friction or hostility between groups of students in our school.	1	2	3	4	5

	Strongly Disagree	Disagree	Neutral	Agree	Strongly Agree
5. New students are made to feel welcome and a part of our school.	1	2	3	4	5

V. STUDENT ACHIEVEMENT/LEARNING ENVIRONMENT

	Strongly Disagree	Disagree	Neutral	Agree	Strongly Agree
1. Student achievement is high in our school.	1	2	3	4	5
2. Students feel that our school program is meaningful.	1	2	3	4	5
3. The teachers in our school make learning enjoyable.	1	2	3	4	5
4. I like who I am and feel good about myself.	1	2	3	4	5
5. Students in our school seem to like and feel good about themselves.	1	2	3	4	5

lected references at the close of this chapter for further reading.

The literature sets forth numerous strategies and provisions for improving the school's climate. The following list represents a synthesis of current literature in this respect.

Characteristics and Provisions for Growth and Renewal. Schools can facilitate a positive climate and creative environment by:

1. Establishing a school focus exemplified by having:

    ♦ a set of shared school goals that serve to direct the program's activities and allocation of fiscal and human resources

    ♦ an organized way of reviewing the school goals with views toward expanding dimensions

    ♦ a set of goals and program objectives unique to the school, its cultural setting, and the needs of its clientele

2. Establishing and maintaining a positive self-image by fostering:

    ♦ personal and school performance expectations that require the best each person can provide

    ♦ an awareness of the school's uniqueness, its cultural assumptions and attitude toward positive change

3. Establishing a program that fosters personal growth by encouraging:

    ♦ strategies that promote constructive self-criticism

    ♦ self-evaluations leading to self-development activities

    ♦ controlled experimentation and having the flexibility to absorb errors that are inevitable in a creative, forward-looking school setting

4. Establishing methods for gaining new and creative ideas by implementing:

    ♦ viable suggestion systems that weigh the value of an idea on the basis of merit rather than the source of the idea

♦ a wide variety of strategies for gaining "best suggestions" for school improvement and problem resolution (e.g., use of think-tank methods, shadow groups, suggestion forums, idea exchange sessions, idea communication channels, etc.).

5. Establishing flexibility in the school's structure by providing:

♦ viable methods of combating vested school/community interests that tend to inhibit positive change

♦ a mentality that looks toward what the school can become as opposed to what it has been

♦ a more diversified involvement in decisions about programs, program changes, and "best solutions"

♦ a "risk-free" atmosphere

6. Establishing a problem-solving capacity within the school by encouraging:

♦ investment in basic, relevant educational research

♦ experimentation and an attitude of questioning the status quo (e.g., What would happen if . . . . ?, Is the present procedure the best one available to us?, etc.)

♦ the utilization, facilitation, and completion of meaningful and relevant research by school personnel

7. Establishing a method for developing, adopting, and implementing a viable set of personnel policies that provides for:

♦ a comprehensive program of human resource services

♦ an effective program of recruiting, selecting, orienting, assigning, and developing the school's human resources

♦ a positive environment for a diversified group of professional personnel

THE PRINCIPAL AT WORK

It is not possible to provide examples for all possible applications of practices set forth in the foregoing discussion. One specific example of an application follows that focuses on the development of a creative school environment by encouraging controlled experimentation and having sufficient flexibility to absorb errors that inevitably occur. Although uncontrolled innovation and experimentation are not advocated, the principal must seek a balance between the freedom to be creative in a risk-free climate and expected accountability. The principal, therefore, must evaluate strategies that will provide opportunities for positive change by implementing "pilot" programs supported by empirical research. New methods, creative approaches, and new programs are piloted, closely monitored, and evaluated against expected outcomes and actual results. A creative climate necessitates an environment that encourages the utilization of individual talents; to achieve this end opportunities to create in a risk-free environment are essential.

HUMAN RESOURCES ALLOCATION AND TEACHER LOAD

Human resources allocation and effective utilization of personnel require that the school administration give full attention to teacher load. There are several important reasons for school administrators to have knowledge and understanding of teacher load information in their schools. Such information is essential in resources allocation in that it serves to:

1) substantiate the actual time allocations that teachers devote to the variety of responsibilities they perform

2) help determine an equitable allocation of teaching and non-teaching duties for teachers in the school

3) provide data for comparing work load assignments among and between teachers, departments, schools and school districts

4) support requests for needed additions to the school staff

5) educate the public as to the comprehensive nature of the work of professional teachers

6) provide data for examining the effects of teacher load on program quality and school improvement.

STRATEGIES FOR DETERMINING THE LOAD OF TEACHERS IN THE SCHOOL

Class size typically is viewed as synonymous with teacher load. Yet, the number of pupils in the classroom is only one major factor of the teacher's work load. Other factors such as the number of classes taught, number of preparations required, specific subjects taught, length of class periods, other grades taught in a single classroom, and extra duty assignments constitute the load of teachers as well.

Intelligent allocation of human resources requires a thorough analysis and understanding of teacher load. Not only does such information permit a better balance in the allocation of human resources, but it serves to obviate inequities that inevitably occur when loads are assigned subjectively. Studies of teacher load have found that the heaviest loads often are assigned to teachers new to the school. Also, unless the principal keeps the equitability of load assignments clearly in mind, those teachers most capable of contributing to school goals often become so overburdened that their contributions are severely decreased.

FORMULAS FOR TEACHER LOAD MEASUREMENT

A commonly utilized formula for measuring teacher load at the high school level is the Douglass Teacher Load Formula (1950). Although the formula was developed several years ago, it has been empirically tested and updated several times throughout the years. It encompasses most all of the factors that comprise the load of secondary school teachers, and its computation results in an index of load that may be compared to existing state and national norms, or to other loads of teachers, schools, and school districts. The formula is as follows:

$$TL = SGC\left[CP - \frac{Dup}{10} + \frac{NP - 25(CP)}{100}\right]\left[\frac{PL + 50}{100}\right] + .6PC\left[\frac{PL + 50}{100}\right]$$

TL = units of teaching load per week

CP = class periods spent in the classroom per week

Dup = number of duplicate class preparations per week

NP = number of pupils in classes per week

PC = periods spent in cooperative duties per week (meetings, supervisory duties, sponsorship, etc.)

PL = length of class periods in minutes

SGC = subject grade coefficient calculated for each subject (SGCs for all subject areas have been calculated; see Douglass, 1951; Jung, 1948).

Figure 5.8 illustrates the application of the Douglass Formula.

With the use of computer technology, the load calculation time for teachers in any school is minimal. Since the Douglass Formula is appropriate for secondary school grades only, the newly developed Norton/Bria Formula (1992) is recommended for measuring teacher load at the elementary school level. The formula is based on the research of Norton, Bria, Frost, Douglass, and others. This formula differs from the Douglass Formula in several ways, but does include most factors that constitute the work load of the elementary school teacher. Unlike the Douglass Formula, the Norton/Bria Formula results in an index of load based on hours and minutes. The Norton/Bria Formula is as follows:

$$THL = 3/2 ATH + \frac{SL \times PH}{CM} + F' \text{ or } F'' (OG \times PH) + .6 (CH)$$

THL = total load index in hours of time per week

ATH = assigned teaching hours in the classroom per week

PH = preparation hours (equivalent to one-half ATH)

SL = actual student number taught above or below the standard class size for a given grade (based on state or local standard norms)

CM = standard class mean size

OG = other grades taught in a single classroom by one teacher (e.g., a teacher who teaches grades 1 and 2 together in one room, OG = 1)

FIGURE 5.8 APPLICATION OF THE DOUGLASS FORMULA

A high school science teacher has five classes of 10th grade biology each day. Class periods are 50 minutes in length. Pupil class enrollments are 28, 31, 23, 28 and 27. During the semester, the teacher averages the equivalent of 4 class periods per week in cooperative assignments. The SGC for high school science is 1.1.

Step 1 - Determine the values for the variables in the Douglass Formula:

SGC = 1.1 for 10th grade science
CP   = 25 (teacher has 5 daily classes and each meets 5
           times a week)
DUP = 20 (teacher has four duplicate preparations five times
           per week. Thus 4 x 5 = 20)
NP   = 28+31+23+28+27 = 137 each day. 137 X 5 days per
           week = 685
PL   = 50 minutes
PC   = 4 class period equivalency per week

Step 2 - Substitute values and perform calculations:

$$TL = 1.1[25 - \frac{20}{10} + \frac{685 - 25(25)}{100}][\frac{50 + 50}{100}] + .6(4)[\frac{50 + 50}{100}] = 28.6 \text{ units}$$

F' =   1/16 for small- and medium-sized school districts

F'' =   1/13 for large school districts

CH   =   hours spent on cooperative duties (e.g., parental conferences, meetings, playground supervision, etc.)

Figure 5.9 presents an application example of the Norton/Bria Formula.

Tools such as the Douglass and Norton/Bria teacher load formulas are readily available to school principals for gathering useful data that facilitate the effective allocation of human resources. In view of the universal opinion that people are the most important resource in the school, the need to give priority attention to teacher load is self-evident.

PLANNING AND ORGANIZING AN EFFECTIVE PROGRAM OF STAFF DEVELOPMENT

The school principal has the primary responsibility for creating a school environment that encourages and facilitates positive personal growth on the part of each staff member. This leadership task includes the responsibility of providing planned development programs that center on relevant learning and skill development which enables the teacher to perform at the level of competency required in current and in expanding position assignments. Staff development, as an integral consideration of resources allocation, must serve the school's primary goals: increasing instructional effectiveness and improving student learning.

A SUCCESSFUL STAFF DEVELOPMENT PROGRAM

A successful program of staff development is *relevant* in that it is founded on the current and projected needs of school personnel and the school program objectives. A successful program is *developmental* in that it emphasizes the building of personal strengths; remedial training does not dominate program activities. A successful staff development program is *individualized*; it is based on meaningful assessments of personnel and personnel roles in the school. Individualization of the program also is

FIGURE 5.9 APPLICATION OF THE NORTON/BRIA FORMULA

An elementary school teacher has 16 5th grade students and 14 6th grade students in one classroom in a medium size school district. Classes begin at 8:45 a.m. and end at 3:15 p.m. Recesses are for 25 minutes, once in the morning and once in the afternoon. Lunch period for the teacher is 30 minutes. Other cooperative duties include faculty meetings, 60 minutes per week; district meetings, 30 minutes per week; coaching intramurals, 180 minutes per week; and parental conferences, 30 minutes per week.

Step 1 - Determine the values for the variables in the Norton/Bria Formula.

ATH = 25 hr., 50 min [6 hr. 30 min. per day X 5 days per week less 5 X 80 min. (recesses and lunch time)] = 25 hr., 50 min.

SL = 2 [Standard class size for grades 5 and 6 is 28. Student load is based on the actual number of students (30) less the average standard class size (28) = 2]

CM = 28 (standard class size mean is 28)

OG = 1 (One grade other than grade five is taught in the same classroom.) OG = 1.

F' = 1/16 (medium sized school district)

CH = 5 hr. (Faculty meetings, 60 min.; district meetings, 30 min.; intramurals, 180 min.; and parental conferences, 30 min. = 300 min. or 5 hr.)

Step 2 - Substitute values in the Norton/Bria Formula and calculate.

$$TLH = 3/2\ (25\ hr.\ 50\ min.) + \frac{2 \times 12\ hr.\ 55\ min.}{28} + 1/6\ (1 \times 2\ hr.\ 55\ min.) + .6(5\ hr.)$$

38 hr. 45 min. + 55 min. + 48 min. + 3 hr. = 43.5 hr.

reflected in the variety of strategies and approaches incorporated into developmental activities and experiences. Finally, a successful staff development program is *continuous*; it is founded on the concept that the school will progress as the individual members of the school staff continue to grow and develop.

Staff development planners and directors must keep in mind that they are working with adult learners. As adult learners, teachers must be viewed as individuals; persons with varying personal needs and interests. Adults must see the relevance of the learning experiences and how the learning will reflect positively in their work as teachers. Also, as adult learners, teachers must be involved in determining their learning objectives and activities in which they will participate.

TRENDS IN PROFESSIONAL STAFF DEVELOPMENT

The foregoing discussion of the characteristics of a successful staff development program suggests several important trends. Figure 5.10 presents the trends that complement a successful program as well.

STAFF DEVELOPMENT OPERATIONAL MODEL

Step 1 - The Guiding Policy for Staff Development is Adopted. Staff development policy, like policy in other governance areas, sets forth the aims for what is to be accomplished. School district policies concerning staff development are adopted by the school board; they not only answer the general question of "what to do?" but typically assign the responsibility for leadership. Figure 5.11 is an example of a staff development policy. Note that the policy sets forth the aim of the staff development program, assigns leadership responsibility, and leaves room for discretionary administrative action for its implementation.

Step 2 - A Statement of Program Goals, Objectives and Guiding Procedures is Determined by the Professional Staff with the Leadership of the School Principal. Staff development goals, objectives, and procedures evolve from the district's staff development policy. Specific program goals and objectives are determined through the cooperative involvement of the school staff. An example of a partial procedural statement of staff development is illustrated in Figure 5.12.

FIGURE 5.10 TRENDS IN PROFESSIONAL STAFF DEVELOPMENT

AWAY FROM	**TOWARD**
Inservice Training	Staff Development
Development As An Event	Development As An Ongoing, Continuous Process
Sporadic and Disorganized Activities	Systematic Strategies and Defined Objectives
Singular Focus	Multi-Faceted Approach
Focus on Remediation	Focus on Personal and School Strengths
Passive Approach - Forced Involvement Based on Reaction to Some Need	Proactive Approach - Self-Initiative Implemented Based on Identified Needs of Present and Future
Isolated Activity	Linked With Other Processes - Orientation, Assignment, Performance Appraisal and Others
Development Ideas Determined Primarily by School Leadership	Development Ideas/Programs Determined Cooperatively by School Leadership, Instructional Teams, Task Force Groups and Others
Ad Hoc, Fragmented Projects	Coordinated Use of Development Models Such As RPTIM (Discussed Later in the Chapter)
Limited Evaluation of Program Results	Comprehensive Self and System Evaluations. Emphasis placed on the Extent to Which Original Objectives Were Realized

---

FIGURE 5.11 STAFF DEVELOPMENT POLICY

Code 4131.1

Continuous personal growth and development are regarded as both an organizational and personal responsibility for all employees of the College View School District. Programs and activities of staff development should be based on the stated objectives of the school's program and the identified personal needs and interests of the school staff. Both short and long range needs of the school staff should be considered in the design and delivery of development programs and activities in order to meet present program needs and to gain competencies required for the future.

Staff development is the primary responsibility of the school superintendent and, in turn, the local school building principal who serves as the leader in planning, designing and implementing staff development programs in cooperation with appropriate staff personnel.

Step 3 - Program Activities and Delivery Systems are Planned and Programmed; Plans and Program Options are Operationalized.

The widely known RPTIM model for staff development (Thompson, 1982) exemplifies the basic procedures that are encompassed in Step 3. The RPTIM model focuses on the following five procedures:

1) *Readiness* - A positive climate is developed, supported by a clear purpose of staff development activities and personnel participation outcomes.

2) *Planning* - Specific goals for the staff development program(s) anticipated are determined; leadership and support are identified.

3) *Training* - Program activities are designed and leadership assignments are determined.

4) *Implementation* - Specific program activities are implemented based on identified program goals and personnel interests.

5) *Maintenance* - Program effectiveness is monitored and altered as necessary.

FIGURE 5.12 STAFF DEVELOPMENT REGULATION (PARTIAL)

Regulation
4910.1

HUMAN RESOURCES

Professional Growth Activities - Certificated Employees

Teachers contemplating professional growth activities are requested to consult with the principal prior to engaging in the activity, for the purpose of ascertaining the feasibility of the activity being planned. This is especially important if there is doubt about the granting of credit for the activity contemplated.

Point System for Accreditment of Activities

Evidence of completed professional growth activities totaling 100 points (tenure staff) or 30 points (probationary staff) must be recorded on the Professional Growth Form. During an annual conference, the staff member and principal/supervisor will review the activities recorded for the year. At the end of the six-year professional growth period, the Professional Growth Form will be signed by the principal/supervisor and staff member to verify completion of the requirement. One copy of the form will be submitted to the Human Resources Office, one copy to the certificated employee and one to the principal/supervisor for the building personnel file.

There are numerous approaches and strategies available to school leaders for the implementation of staff development. A few selected strategies are as follows:

- **Quality Circles** - Placing the primary responsibility for personal growth upon individuals linked together for purposes of improvement.

- **Teacher Centers** - An empirical environment of resources, personal involvement, and peer communication for purposes of individual growth.

- **Peer-Assisted Leadership** - A self-reflection process that uses interviewing, shadowing, and reflective feedback to enhance personal introspection and development.

- **Assessment Centers** - A series of activities in which staff members are observed and specific skills are assessed with performance feedback provided.

- **Others** - A partial list would include classes, conferences, field visitations, teacher exchanges, demonstrations, workshops, travel, independent study.

Step 4 - Evaluation of the Staff Development Process is Completed; Program Changes and Improvements are Discussed and Implemented as Determined Necessary. As is noted, Step 4 parallels the maintenance step set forth previously in the RPTIM model. Effective staff evaluation programs necessitate careful monitoring and critical evaluation. Evaluation focuses on the extent to which program goals are achieved. This approach is more concerned with the behavioral changes that take place following the staff development program than with such things as attendance, interest in the sessions, and the personalities of the program presenters. For example, let's assume that one objective of a special development program is to extend the use of school/community resources in classroom instruction. Evaluators of the program likely would be interested in gathering follow-up data relative to such questions as:

1) To what extent have the library/media services within the school increased since the completion of the staff development program?

2) Has the utilization of community resources in the areas of science, social studies, and other subject areas been increased since the completion of the staff development program?

3) How has the utilization of school/community resources been evidenced in curriculum revisions that have occurred since the completion of the staff development program?

Although such program considerations as the numbers attending development programs and the extent to which programs were "enjoyable" for participants are of interest, program effectiveness cannot be viewed as positive unless the program results in positive behavioral changes that lead to desirable program goals.

Thus a successful staff development program is founded on four specific steps:

1) determining and adopting a staff development policy that guides the program

2) developing program goals, objectives, and guiding procedures

3) planning program activities and program delivery systems and their implementation

4) controlling the program through the implementation of an evaluation process that focuses on the extent to which program objectives are achieved.

SUMMARY

The effective allocation of human resources extends from the initial processes of recruitment and selection of quality personnel to the best deployment of human talent, the most efficient and effective assignment of human resources, the assessment of school roles and factors that facilitate and/or inhibit human performance, the establishment of a positive environment within the school setting, and the provisions for meaningful work and personal development.

Staff orientation activities, the assignment of personnel, designated staffing patterns, school climate, work load and working conditions, and staff development constitute the major processes and factors through which effective human resources allocation takes place. Staff orientation has a primary purpose of introducing new staff personnel to their responsibilities in the school and the community. Its significance has been emphasized by research studies that link orientation practices to teacher morale. Staff orientation serves to gain congruency between the school's goals and employee needs. Orientation includes four steps as follows:

1) the establishment of personnel orientation policies
2) the identification of orientation program needs and the planning of programs and responsibilities
3) the implementation of orientation plans
4) the evaluation of program results.

The assignment of personnel to their respective positions and duties centers on the placement of people where there is optimal productive job performance and personal satisfaction. Leadership actions required of the school principal include:

1) the development of an assignment policy to direct the procedure
2) the deployment of staff talent in the best interests of all concerned
3) the assignment of personnel to facilitate school staffing and instructional programming
4) the development of a positive working climate that fosters the maximization of human potential.

Organizational climate is the school atmosphere as characterized by the social and professional interactions of the individuals in the school. Its significance is vested in its influence on school program outcomes. Human resources allocation requires that school leaders understand the nature and importance of school climate, how to assess the climate of the school, and effective strategies for improving it.

The allocation of resources also requires attention to teacher load. Unless the school principal gives teacher load due consideration, inequities are inevitable. Those teachers most capable of outstanding performance often are overloaded and their work efforts reduced to an average performance. Such tools as the Douglass Teacher Load Formula and the Norton/Bria Formula can be instrumental in determining the current load of teachers, including inequities in both teaching and cooperative load assignments.

Finally, human resources allocation requires school leadership that results in staff renewal. A successful staff development program is based on current and projected needs of school personnel and the objectives of the school program. Staff development leadership must focus on:

1) the establishment of a guiding policy for staff development

2) the development of a statement of program goals, objectives, and guiding procedures

3) the planning and implementation of staff development program activities and delivery systems

4) the evaluation of the staff development program for the primary purpose of future program improvement.

FOLLOW-UP ACTIVITIES

1. Schedule a conference with staff personnel who are relatively new to the school. Informally ascertain their opinions about the effectiveness of orientation procedures they experienced in the district and the school. What practices were especially beneficial to them? What recommendations might they have for improving the orientation program in the future?

2. Develop an appropriate form or use the form in Figure 5.3 to survey school faculty personnel on teaching assignments. Examine the survey results relative to present teaching and extra-curricular assignments and stated staff interests. What changes might be in order?

3. Develop a brief climate assessment survey instrument or use the instrument in Figure 5.7 in your school setting. Implement objective procedures to gain input from your staff concerning school climate conditions.

4. Use the Douglass Teacher Load Formula or the Norton/Bria Formula to determine the load of each teacher in the school. Examine load differences relative to new and experienced teachers, cooperative load data, differences among the various subject areas or grade levels, and other results.

REFERENCES

Barnard, C. I. (1938). *The Functions of the Executive*. Cambridge, MA: Harvard University Press.

Bentley, R. R., & Rempel, A. M. (1970). *The Purdue Teacher Opinionaire*. West Lafayette, Indiana: Purdue Research Foundation, Purdue University.

Berglas, W. W. (1973). A Study of the Relationship Between Induction Practices and the Morale of the Beginning Teacher. *Dissertation Abstracts International*, 34(5), 2189-A.

Christian, C. F. (1972). Organizational Climate of Elementary Schools and the Introduction and Utilization of Innovative Educational Practices. Unpublished doctoral dissertation, University of Nebraska, Lincoln.

Coil, A. (1984). Job Matching Brings Out the Best in Employees. *Personnel Journal*, 63(1), 54–60.

Douglass, H. R. (1951). The 1950 Revision of the Douglass High School Teaching Load Formula. *The Bulletin*, 35(179), 13–24.

Drucker, P. E. (1974). *Management, Tasks, Responsibilities, Practices*. New York: Harper & Row.

Frost, N. (1941). What Teaching Load? *American School Board Journal*, 102(3), 42–43.

Halpin, A. W., & Croft, D. B. (1963). *The Organizational Climate of Schools*. Chicago: Midwest Administration Center, The University of Chicago.

Hoy, W. K., & Forsyth, P. B. (1986). *Effective Supervision*. New York: Random House.

Hughes, L. W., & Ubben, G. C. (1989). *The Elementary Principal's Handbook* (3rd ed.). Boston: Allyn & Bacon.

Jung, C. W. (1949). The Development of a Proposed Revision of the Douglass Formula for Measuring Teacher Load in the Secondary School. Unpublished Doctoral Dissertation, University of Colorado, Boulder.

Knezevich, S. J. (1975). *Administration of Public Education* (3rd ed.). New York: Harper & Row, Publishers.

Norton, M. S., & Bria, R. (1992, Fall/Winter). Toward an Equitable Measure of Elementary School Teacher Load. *Record*, 62–66.

Stern, G. G. (1964). *High School Characteristics Index*. Syracuse, NY: Psychological Research Center, Syracuse University.

Thompson, S. R. (1982). A Survey and Analysis of Pennsylvania Public School Personnel Perceptions of Staff Development Practices and Beliefs with a View to Identifying Some Critical Problems or Needs. Unpublished doctoral dissertation, Pennsylvania State University, State College.

SUGGESTED READINGS

Castetter, W. B. (1996). *The Human Resource Function in Educational Administration* (6th ed.). Englewood Cliffs, New Jersey: Prentice Hall, Inc.

Norton, M. S. (1987). Employee Assistance Programs in Education. *Contemporary Education*, 60, 23–26.

Rumsey, M. J. (1992). Making EAP Referrals Work. *EAP Digest*, 12(5), 42–43.

Seaman, D. F., & Fellenz, R. A. (1989). *Effective Strategies for Teaching Adults*. New York: Merrill/Macmillan.

Webb, L. D., Montello, P. A., & Norton, M. S. (1994). *Human Resources Administration* (2nd ed.). New York: Merrill, An imprint of Macmillan Publishing Company.

Woodhall, M. (1987). Human Capital Concepts. In G. Psacharopoulos (Ed.), *Economics of Education: Research and Studies* (pp. 21–24). Oxford, England: Pergamon.